WHAT'S RIGHT?

A Teenager's Guide to Christian Living

Jim Auer

LIGUORI
PUBLICATIONS

One Liguori Drive
Liguori, Missouri 63057
(314) 464-2500

Imprimi Potest:
Stephen T. Palmer, C.SS.R.
Provincial, St. Louis Province
Redemptorist Fathers

Imprimatur:
+ Edward J. O'Donnell
Vicar General, Archdiocese of St. Louis

ISBN 0-89243-265-9
Library of Congress Catalog Card Number: 86-83164

Table of Contents

Seven: The (Shhh!) You-Know-What Part

Eight: On the Home Front

Nine: You Don't Live in a Vacuum

Ten: *Honestly!* (That's a Good Idea!)

Eleven: Other Folks — They Live Here, Too

Twelve: Saint _____

(Please Print Clearly) Yes, *You!*

Thirteen: Let's Try to Bring It All Together

SECTION ONE:
LIFE
(WHY START
SMALL?)

1. Let's See ... You're Worth About?

Most shows start with commercials, right? Imagine this one, then. The scene is a supermarket exit. A man in a suit and tie is about to approach a lady leaving with a cart full of groceries. Of course she doesn't know there's a hidden camera in the bubble gum machine by the door.

Man: Ma'am? I see you have a box of Slosho-With-Suds-Buds in this grocery bag.

Lady: Of course. I've used Slosho for years.

Man: We'd like to take away your Slosho for a month and have you use this other brand. How about it?

Lady: *Aaaachhh!* A whole month without Slosho? Thirty dirty, grimy days without the miracle cleaning action of Suds-Buds? No way! Just the idea is making me sick. Quick — somebody bring me something with thirty-three percent more active pain reliever!

You've probably seen commercials with this "No way, I'd never switch to a different brand" gimmick. The commercials may be pure silliness, but the gimmick is based on a principle that really is true: You often don't appreciate something until you either lose it or come very close to losing it.

I have a terrific daughter named Jeannie. It's safe to say I've never stopped loving her or being glad she's my daughter. But I appreciate her more every time I remember the night several years ago when she disappeared and got lost in a huge shopping mall. When we finally found her, sobbing but safe, every single thing about her seemed twice as wonderful as before. More than ever I appreciated her laughter and her curls and just having her here and alive as my kid.

Some people are lucky enough to almost get killed (without getting hurt). For example, you step into the street without looking and this huge bus grinds to a stop right before it would have flattened you into a piece of cardboard, like on the Saturday morning cartoons.

So, some people are lucky to have an experience like this. It makes them aware of the inmost basic and most wonderful gift: *life*. Because it's so basic, you usually don't think about it much, just as you're seldom aware of other ground-level things like air and food and water. Plus all the things you can *do* because you're alive.

Would you take a million dollars for your eyesight? That's a million bucks, tax-free, all yours to spend any way you want . . . except that you'll never be able to see what you bought — or anything else.

How about your hearing? A million dollars for your hearing? How about *five* million for your ability to move — would you agree to be permanently paralyzed in return for five million?

Would you consider ten million, no ten *billion* — dollars in exchange for your consciousness . . . your ability to think and imagine and decide? Would you agree to lie in a permanent coma for ten billion?

If your answers are "no," then you keep your multi-billionaire's worth of a living, breathing, seeing, hearing, moving, thinking humanity.

And there's much more: God has filled your life with grace, with *his* life, which means you can live forever in perfect happiness unless you really spoil things by the way you live here on earth.

A few years ago, a certain beer commercial enticed you with words similar to these: "You only go around once, so live your life with gusto. Reach for a _____ ." That's not a bad suggestion, although living with gusto doesn't mean you have to buy that particular beer or any kind of beer. But there's a better way to complete that slogan: "You only go around once — and your eternity depends on how you do it."

You can start by really appreciating and giving thanks for the gift of life. If you're aware of how precious it is, you won't be so likely to mess it up.

Want to try a wild experiment? Go alone somewhere, relax, and take ten slow, deep breaths, being very aware of each one. And then say thanks — actually say it. Take ten steps, being very conscious of your legs moving at each step. Say thanks again. Pick out an object in the room or wherever you are and study its shape and color and texture. Tune in to whatever sounds are around you. Once more, say thanks. You've just done some things many people can't do. You've enjoyed part of your multibillion dollar account in the Bank of Humanity — without using it up.

That's good reason for saying thanks.

2. The Ultimate Game Show Question

Pretend that you are in attendance at a game show television program. But you are not just watching it; you've made it as a contestant. You stand on the stage, bathed in hot, carbon arc lights, surrounded by flashing, multicolored bulbs and wildly blinking scoreboards. You've answered question after question. You've gone farther than any previous contestant in game show history and now there's one question left. Answer this one and you win five new cars, trips to Hawaii, Tahiti, London, and Paris, two households full of custom furniture, a fluorescent orange grand piano, a heart-shaped swimming pool, fourteen sets of luggage, twenty-five pounds of designer paper clips, three million dollars, and a year's supply of creme rinse and dog food.

Your final question will obviously be special. The ever-smiling game show host hands it to you on a textured white card with glossy black engraving. The card reads: "Why are you here on earth?"

OK, the situation is a bit of fantasy. But the question is worth thinking about. What would you answer?

"Because my mom and dad had a kid."

That covers basic biology, but it's not very much into the idea of purpose. Again, the question, "Why are you here on earth?"

"To take out the garbage, dry dishes, pass my impossible math classes, provide gym class with a little comedy when it comes to rope climbing, and give that cute exchange student a reason for staying in this country." These plug into the idea of purpose and the last one even gets interesting, but you can sense that none of them comes halfway close to being the bottom line.

Of course, some people would answer, "Who cares?" or "What difference does it make?" That's the "Who cares where you're supposed to go — just drive . . . and party as much as you can along the way!" approach.

Some people can make it sound attractive, even convincing. They seem to make a decent case that life can't be figured out anyway, so there's no sense trying. You only go around once, so live with gusto. You'll find out what it was all about soon enough when you die.

This can even sound sort of daring and independent: "Look, man — I live hard, play hard, and let the cards fall where they fall, you know. If they don't fall where they were supposed to, tough."

That may *sound* cool, but the way things sound isn't always the way things *are*. The "What do I care?" approach to the meaning of life is a lot more dumb than it is daring. If somebody put you here, that somebody had a reason and it's not particularly smart to tune that reason out or to refuse to look for it.

"Why are you here on earth?"

Back when the first game shows were really big on TV, contestants were sometimes allowed to have a guest expert help them answer the top-level questions. Maybe you should bring in some guest experts on this one, people who have thought deeply about life — including a certain carpenter from Nazareth.

The carpenter from Nazareth — who was also the Son of God and our Savior — put it this way: "Love the Lord your God . . . love your neighbor as yourself." You were put here by God, who *is* love, as the First Letter of John tells you. Your purpose is to channel and spread the love that you came from.

So now you have the answer . . . it's *that simple*.

Yes.

Well . . . the answer is simple enough. Living out the answer day by day is not always so simple. For one thing, lots of stuff goes around advertised as love when it's not. Love means that you do what is really, genuinely good for somebody else.

Sometimes that can practically give you a high. OK. Enjoy and be grateful. But lots of times it won't. Sometimes loving means doing things that are difficult, things you're not crazy about — even things the person you love isn't crazy about and doesn't appreciate a bit at the time.

I'm not giving you the classic cop out on a relationship with God himself. You've probably heard it: "You don't have to actually think much about God and pray to him and all that stuff — just be nice to people." You very much need a one-on-one relationship with God. If you don't have a loving relationship with God, it's very easy to flunk out of loving people.

But in much of your daily life God has chosen to relate with you through other people. If you're asking, "Where's God — I'd like to do something so he knows I love him," God has already answered that question: "Do you see a human being anywhere around? That's me. Do something good."

There are two opposite mistakes to avoid: (1) thinking that something comes from love when it really comes more from a selfish interest; (2) overlooking ordinary things that may not bring a fantastic warm glow, like doing dishes and running errands, but which are genuinely acts of love. Jesus, remember, used simply getting somebody a drink of water as an example of love.

3. The Talk Show Looks at Life

"Good evening — and welcome once again to *Conversational Junque,*
America's most exciting interview and talk show! I'm Harvey Verbose,
your host, and with us tonight are two professional airline pilots. Each is
going to give his personal view of what it's like to pilot one of those big
monsters through the sky. First, let's talk with this man on my right,
Captain D. Preston Pheerful. Which airline are you with, Captain?"

"I'm with Morbid Sky Systems, Harv. At least for now."

"Why do you say 'for now,' Captain?"

"Well, you never know. Next time up I might get off my flight pattern
and drive the thing into a mountain. Bang and it's all over."

"Do you think about this much?"

"Sure. See, I make lots of mistakes."

"You do?"

"All the time, Harv, all the time. Just yesterday, for example, I brought
Flight 2310 nonstop from London to Chicago, and you know what? I
forgot to stand by the exit and thank the passengers for flying with us."

"Well, I don't think that's too —"

"My boss is probably thinking about firing me right now. I can't
blame him. Man, I wish I wasn't such a lousy pilot."

"I see . . . well, let's uh . . . come back to you Captain and go to our
other guest for a change of pace. This is Captain Charlie Goodtimes.
You're with Wide Open Airspace, is that correct?"

"You got it, Harv. We're known as the Fly *Real* High people."

"How did you get that slogan, Captain?"

"Well, Harv, we believe the good old atmosphere up there is for havin'
fun. That's what my flights are all about."

"Don't you have a destination — someplace definite where you're
supposed to land the plane?"

"Oh, sure, but I don't get hung up on it. That would make it all boring,
man! Once I'm up in the air, I do a few loops and rolls and some other
kinky stuff for kicks. Then I hit the autopilot and go back and party with
the passengers."

"Captain Goodtimes, couldn't the autopilot take you into the side of a mountain, as Captain Pheerful mentioned?"

"Oh . . . I guess it could. I don't like to think about that stuff, though. Besides, it's never happened. Yet. Why worry about something until it happens?"

Fortunately, there are no airline pilots like either of them. If you had to choose between those two, no doubt you'd stay on the ground.

Captain Pheerful is so hung up on rehashing his past mistakes that he might not even *see* a mountain a hundred yards in front of him. Listen as he talks to the passengers: "We've got real bad weather ahead, folks — real bad. There's a good chance we won't make it." Some of his passengers might decide they'd have a better chance if they jumped out of the plane in midtrip.

Captain Goodtimes might provide a thrill or two along the way. But what about the cost of those temporary thrills? Jet flights are supposed to be enjoyable, but you're also supposed to get somewhere. That's why you're on the plane. And it's a nice idea to get there with your arms and legs functioning and your general health in good shape. With him in charge, you couldn't be too sure of that.

Captain Pheerful cares about what he does, but in the wrong way. He thinks only about mistakes, both real ones and ones he's afraid he might make. Captain Goodtimes doesn't care, not about the important things anyway. His plane splits through miles of airspace, but he doesn't pay much attention to where it's heading, or check that all the systems are operating correctly. Our two imaginary captains are opposites.

They illustrate opposite ways of looking at how you should conduct your life. You are in charge of a flight toward eternity. You are your own pilot. How much do you care about how the flight is going? Chances are you're not as extreme as either of our imaginary captains. But you can learn from their opposite ways of looking at things.

If you figure that you're just no good at this business of being Christian and probably never will be, you're tuning out God's forgiveness and help. On the other hand, if you never bother to examine your life or just don't care whether you're acting as you should or not, you're tuning out the whole idea of being a Christian at all.

There's a better way to go. It involves realizing two things: (1) God will forgive any mistakes you've ever done or ever will do; (2) God does expect you to play it straight, to do the best you can with what you have at any time.

SECTION TWO:
THIS RELIGION STUFF

4. And It Looked So Pretty on the Outside

It's your birthday, and you're not expecting the world and all it's treasures but . . . well, it's your birthday. A little something would be in order, right? Right.

So, in the morning you come down from your room and on the table is a very nicely wrapped package with your name on the tag. It's from somebody you expect a present from: mom, dad, brother, sister, friend, Aunt Josephine in Buffalo.

You pick up the box. It feels pretty light, but that adds to the mystery. You shake it, but nothing rattles or even rustles. The mystery deepens. So you rip off the wrapping paper, break the tape, open the package, and it's . . . empty. Just plain empty. Except for a little piece of paper at the bottom that says "Happy Birthday" in black, generic letters. It's signed by the one who sent the package. Well, sort of signed. The signature was put on with a rubber stamp copied from the person's handwriting.

That's it. Empty box, heap of wrapping paper, and a generic note signed with a rubber stamp. Did you get a birthday package? Sure. It even looked pretty decent on the outside.

Did you get a birthday *present?* Did the package *mean* anything? Dumb questions.

The present didn't have to be a diamond necklace or round trip tickets to Hawaii with all expenses paid or lifetime tickets to the Super Bowl. But it should have been *something* or why call it a present? Even something very little would have been fine with a note saying, "I'm sorry — I mean to give you something more when I'm able, but this is really the best I can do right now. Please accept it." You couldn't possibly be upset with anyone for that kind of honesty.

Religion is like that.

If there's nothing *inside you* in your relationship with God, well, then there isn't much of a relationship.

You can say all kinds of things in front of other people. You can give all the right answers: "Sure-man-I-believe-in-God-and-Jesus-he-died-on-the-cross-for-us-ain't-that-cool-and-we-gotta-save-our-souls-and-get-to-heaven and so forth." Just to say all that doesn't cost you anything. You can even bring your body inside a church on Sunday morning. That costs a little bit, but not too much.

You can do all that and still be like the birthday "present" — the box that was empty on the inside. That box and the wrapping paper cost a little bit — but not much — and didn't mean anything. If there's nothing *inside you,* there's no sense in calling it religion — any more than calling the empty box a present. Maybe it's habit or maybe it's keeping peace with your parents or something like that. But not religion.

So what *is* religion — where does it begin?

Religion begins with knowing that you didn't start yourself, that you didn't have the power to keep yourself going forever, and that in the meantime you can't always hack it and make sense of stuff by yourself. Even on days when you feel on top of the world, if you're smart you know it doesn't explain the universe and it won't last. Maybe you come through with a B in biology, buy three new albums, and order a large pizza with extra everything. A "little voice" should tell you, "Yeah, terrific, but sooner or later you're gonna forget about that B, the groups who made the albums probably won't even be together a few years from now, and the pizza won't be around more than twenty minutes. Then what?"

Religion begins with looking around at the world, at things going on around you, and realizing, "All this didn't just start itself, this doesn't make sense by itself. Somebody made this." And then you realize that the Somebody who made all this must still stand behind the scenes of this confusing, billion-act live drama called Daily Life in the Universe.

And finally you realize, "I have to *do something* about that. I have to recognize the Somebody who's in charge. I have to find out what this ball game is about and how I should act to make things turn out right."

That Somebody is called "God."

Realizing that you are God's creation, that God must care about you, and that you have to respond to this and learn to act as you should because of it — that's religion. At least that's where it starts. Notice that it's inside you. Without an inside, remember, the outside doesn't mean much.

Pray about it. Your prayer doesn't have to be fancy, either.

"God, I know you're in charge of all this. I need you. I want to turn out like you planned. Help me do what I need to do."

5. Letters to the Wise One

Dear Wise One,

I've been going with this boy . . . well, sort of going with him. I really like him, but I have a problem. He *says* he likes me, but he doesn't pay much attention to me. Sometimes two weeks go by and he doesn't even call (unless he needs help preparing for a test). Last week was my birthday. He knew it and didn't even send a card or call me. It's not like I was expecting a diamond necklace, but total zero really hurt. When I told him this, he said he was thinking of me on my birthday and it's the thought that counts. What do you think?

Ignored Too Often

Dear Wise One,

I have a problem with my parents. They say they're so concerned about how I do in school, and that it's important for me to get good grades. But when I bring home good papers, they hardly notice. I don't expect ten bucks for every A or something like that, but a little attention would be nice. And when I could use some help studying for a test, they're always too busy.

One-Way Street

Dear Wise One,

This isn't exactly a big problem, but I want to know what you think. My friend says she's really into art and that it's a big thing in her life. She's always talking about how she loves "creating." Well, I was at her home the other day and asked to see some things she's done. I was really interested. But there weren't any. No paintings, no ceramics, no weaving, no anything. She said she hadn't gotten around to starting any yet. Why do people put on a big act like that?

Just Wondering

There's a common thread in all these situations, isn't there? Something that's supposed to be on the *inside* just isn't showing up on the *outside*.

16

You already know, of course, that if there's nothing on the inside, the outside doesn't make much difference. That's still true. This is the other side of the coin.

Picture a stadium full of people at a sports event. What would you think if they never cheered, booed, yelled, clapped, or waved their arms? Can you imagine a team that wanted to get to the finals but never designed any plays and seldom even practiced?

This violates your sense of how things ought to be. You usually judge the intensity and the sincerity of people's feelings and ideas by *what they do about them*. Not just how much they say — what they do.

It doesn't even mean they have to succeed at what they attempt. It's how often and how hard they try. If somebody practices golf three times a week and enters a tournament fourteen years in a row but never wins, you still know that winning the tournament is important to that person, even if it never happens. He or she is obviously sincere about *wanting* to win.

A stadium full of people who come to watch their team win but never do anything, never even make any noise . . . if you were there, you'd get a real uneasy feeling, wouldn't you? You'd say, "This is strange . . . too strange. Something's wrong. These people aren't real."

What about believing in a God who created you and has a plan for you, believing there's a life after death, knowing there's such a thing as good and evil . . . but *not doing anything about it?*

That's no different. Now God doesn't expect you to have your mind on him all the time. He doesn't expect you to get as cranked up over reading the Acts of the Apostles as you do over a game-winning touchdown or a surprise invitation to the prom from the person of your dreams.

But your faith has to have an outside expression of what you believe on the inside. That's the way human beings are. If something matters to you, it shows — you express it, you do things, you act in certain ways because of it.

This inside-outside aspect of you is so closely connected that if you stop doing something on the outside, you tend to lose the part that used to be inside. For example, if a close friend moves far away and you can no longer share music and movies, pizza and problems and conversations, for a while there's a big empty spot and it may even seem like you're closer than ever because you miss the other person so much. But after some time passes, it's difficult to have the same intense feelings that you formerly had for that person. It doesn't mean that love has turned to hate. It's just that ideas and feelings and beliefs that aren't expressed tend to fade away and finally evaporate.

"*My* religion is in my heart, see. I don't need to go to church and say prayers and keep all kinds of rules."

Does that make sense? Listen to Ignored's boyfriend. He tells her, "Sweetheart, my feeling for you is in my heart. I don't need to call you and talk to you a lot or go places with you or give you presents on special occasions. That's just all on the outside. As long as I'm thinking of you on the inside, that's what counts."

You have some idea of what she ought to tell him, don't you?

It's the same with your faith, your religion. There has to be something on the inside. But if it doesn't show very much, if you don't do anything about it, maybe there *isn't* much on the inside . . . and then you need to work on that.

6. It's All So, Like, Y'Know, Phony

You've probably seen professional wrestling. If you haven't, please don't feel deprived. Even if you haven't seen it, you've probably heard people talk about it. You probably know that most matches feature a good guy, a bad guy, the bad guy's manager, and a referee.

The good guy keeps the rules — until the bad guy makes him really mad. Even then he doesn't break them as badly as the bad guy. The bad guy breaks all the rules about every thirty seconds, and hundreds of people see these horrible violations even from the back of the auditorium. The referee, who is a couple feet away, doesn't. Except once in a great while. Then, if it's something really awful, the referee will take drastic action, such as shaking his finger in the bad guy's face and telling him he mustn't be naughty anymore. The bad guy's manager walks around being obnoxious and stirring up the crowd's hatred and distracting the referee so the bad guy can break more rules.

People who don't believe in miracles should watch professional wrestling. At least two or three times in an evening's lineup, a good guy will be very close to permanent coma from all the nasty, illegal stuff the bad guy has been doing (which the referee didn't see). Then suddenly he'll get sort of reincarnated, bounce off the ropes, turn into a human torpedo, and pin the bad guy to the mat or toss him out of the ring.

"Most of that stuff is fake," a lot of people say. No kidding. But you have to be careful about statements like, "Wrestling is phony" and "Wrestling is stupid." That's not accurate or fair. Just because "professional" wrestling is more a big show than a sport, not all wrestling is like that. High school and college and Olympic wrestling is a completely different matter.

It's dangerous to generalize, to see a few cases of phoniness and then say, "The whole thing is phony." If two policemen are found guilty of taking bribes, some people will say, "Yeah, I bet most cops are on the take." If an investigation shows that a couple of athletes took money to "throw" a game, some people will say, "Y'know, I bet half those games are fixed before the guys ever come out of the locker room."

Phony wrestlers, phony policemen, phony athletes, phony anybodies can give all their colleagues a bad name. Nobody likes a hypocrite.

But if you're level-headed and fair, you'll realize that even though a few people in a group may be hypocrites, it doesn't mean they all are. And it doesn't mean that the whole idea the group tries to follow is stupid or unworkable.

The same thing happens when people see phony Christians — or Christians they think are phony. You've probably heard it: "Yeah, sure, just look at the hypocrites coming to church. Every Sunday the church is full of 'em. Then during the week they go out and lie and cheat and tear each other apart. Lotta good all that religion and going to church did for them. Religion is all so phony."

Oh, come on. "All?" *All* those people who come to church — each one has been checked out and found to be a hypocrite?

Some people go around deliberately looking for "phony spots" in something Christian. They love it when they can find a priest who drinks too much or a nun who often loses her temper or a choir director who cheated a bit on an income tax return. Then they can say, "*See* — told you! It's all so phony!"

Notice what a convenient "reason" they now have for dismissing religion in general. It's like they're saying, "Show me you have a perfect society. Then maybe we'll join." That's not fair.

As for people who do have a tendency to lie and cheat and tear each other apart, church is exactly where they should be. Maybe sometime soon they'll find the courage to stop doing those things. Jesus himself said that healthy people don't need a doctor — sick people do.

7. To Ask or Not to Ask? That Is the Question

Chris and I have some great conversations, particularly when I'm in my driveway about to leave. They're fairly predictable, but they're fun.

"Way-yah you go-un, Unca Jim?" Chris is two and a half years old. He lives next door. I'm not actually his uncle, but I like being an adoptive one.

"I'm going to the post office, Chris."

"Why?"

"I have to mail a manuscript."

"Why?"

"Because it's due in three days."

"Why?"

"Because that's when I agreed to have it finished."

"Why?"

As you may have picked up, this can go on for a while. But sooner or later Chris will say "Oh" in a tone that seems to indicate, "*Now* I get it." Then we begin a second series: "When you go-un be baa-yuck?"

Sometimes adults are impatient with kids without meaning to be when it comes to answering questions, so I try to have time for his questions. (It doesn't always work out; sometimes I have to say, "Sorry, Chris, gotta leave now — later.")

And sometimes adults can give the impression that a smart kid or a sensible kid or a good kid wouldn't have asked the question you just asked. It can happen when the topic is religion. Even though they say "If you don't understand something, *ask questions*," some questions seem upsetting. (I have an inside angle on this — I've been teaching for almost twenty years.)

For example, a teacher has just finished a statement — or maybe a five-minute presentation — which began with "Now our faith teaches us that. . . . " But you have a question.

21

Maybe it's "Why?" or "Who says?" or "How do you know?" or "But isn't that just somebody's opinion?"

With honest sincerity on both sides — yours and the adult's — this kind of situation can lead to growth for both you and the adult you've asked.

Sometimes, though, this kind of situation can turn out badly.

1. The adult figures you're simply a smart-mouthed kid and gives a smart-mouthed answer back: "If you don't like it, go join the atheists and go straight to hell without passing GO or collecting two hundred dollars."

2. You decide that this whole religion thing doesn't make much sense, never will, and might as well be scrapped.

3. You get the feeling that really good people don't have questions or problems like yours, so you must not be very good and God is probably a little upset with you for even having the question.

You're not wrong or even a little brazen for questioning some of the things that adults seem to think are pretty well settled. God is not sitting up in heaven thinking, "Wow, I wish all my creatures were like _____ . She accepts everything I've ever said. No problems, no doubts. Really great kid. But that (insert your name), now there is a hard case. He has doubts about practically everything. He'd better shape up his faith act because it's getting awfully hard to like him." If you're having real problems with some things in your faith, God knows they're real problems and he wants to help you work through them, not bust you for having them.

But you owe it to yourself (and to God, obviously) to give yourself what might be called a "gut-honest sincerity check." It goes like this: *Am I really having a hard time making sense out of this . . . or am I sort of looking for an easy excuse out of a religious obligation?* Now that's a tough question to ask; it takes some guts to ask it of yourself. But you should because human beings need to keep themselves honest.

And remember that just because something doesn't make perfect sense to you right now, that doesn't mean that it's stupid and deserves to be tossed out with the leftover pizza crusts. There was a time, remember, when some of the rules and strategies of baseball, soccer, and so forth, didn't make perfect sense to you either.

It should also be mentioned that you don't have to have a storage room full of questions and doubts. The faith journey doesn't follow a set script complete with stage directions that goes something like this: "Well, I'm fifteen years old now so it's time to have a religious crisis and start questioning everything. A lot of my friends are doing that so I'd better do it, too."

If you don't have any heavy doubts or questions right now, fine. Why *look* for static, you know? And if you do have doubts and questions, that's also fine. God will work with you, no matter what direction your growth in faith might take.

But give God a chance to work with you. Don't toss out the whole religion package just because you had a hard time untying one of the ribbons.

SECTION THREE:
CHECKING IN

8. .69444 Percent

Got a little time? I really mean a *little*. Less than one percent of the time in your life. To be exact, *.69444 percent* of your total time per day. That's not a whole lot, right? You wouldn't have to skip any meals, give up any sleep, rush your homework, or even talk with your friends any less. You could give .69444 percent of your day to something, couldn't you?

(I presume that look on your face means yes.)

That tiny bit of time will be returned to in a minute. In the meantime, imagine this character with the classic name of Lancelot.

Lancelot goes to East Central High West. Well, *usually* he does — he cuts a few classes here and there. He's in the ninth grade. He would have been in the tenth; but, well, he's cut some classes here and there and he's bombed on exams now and then and he's missed out on some skills he could use. He's not a total burnout. He's just made some mistakes and they're showing up.

Lancelot is sitting in English One this morning, wishing he were at a movie or a pizza place instead. An announcement comes over the PA. The *state superintendent of education* is visiting the school and would like to meet with a few students individually. Just to talk. One-on-one. It's completely voluntary. Nobody has to go. But if you want to, the opportunity to talk with *the* person in charge is there.

What about it, Lance? Are you going?

"*Me?* Don't freak me out, man. No way."

Why not?

"You gotta be kidding! For one thing, it'll be a drag. He'll be boring. Somebody that important isn't interested in normal life, you know? I couldn't talk about real stuff; I'd have to make up phony words, and I hate that. Besides, he'll probably have all my school records."

Is that a problem, Lance?

"Are you trying to be funny? Yeah, you might say that's a little problem. I'm not exactly your A-1, Johnny Wonderful Student, you know. He'll probably know all that, and it's a little embarrassing. Not that

I care that much about it, but I just don't need anybody on my case. I can't hack somebody telling me how different I should be."

But Lance — the guy has a reputation for being pretty cool to deal with. Some kids who have talked with him have really been changed.

"Yeah, I know — and that's another thing. He might mess with my mind and turn me into a freak. I might actually start liking English and math and all that stuff. Can you imagine what my friends would say?"

He's never been known to brainwash anybody, Lance.

"Yeah, but he still might get to me. I might do something really stupid, like promise to straighten out, or get a B in World History. And then I'd feel like I'd really have to change, and. . . . "

And *what,* Lance?

"That's *scary,* man."

You're probably not exactly like Lance, but sometimes there's a little bit of him in everyone. Especially when you approach the idea of praying. Sometimes the reasons why you don't pray (or don't pray very much or don't really pray from the heart) are similar to Lance's reasons for not wanting to talk with the superintendent.

You're afraid of being bored. You don't like using words that seem unreal. But you're also uncomfortable about using words and ideas from your real, gut-level, daily life. You figure God either wouldn't approve of that or isn't really interested in it.

And you're conscious of your past failings and present weaknesses. You may even imagine God saying, "You've got a lot of nerve coming here to talk with me after all you've done!"

And you're afraid that if you *really* got into prayer regularly and very seriously, God would change you. Or — worse yet — he might make you *want* to change but stick you with the job of doing it!

But there's no record of anybody who got trapped in prayer, wanted to get out but couldn't, and ended up miserable. Miserable, unhappy people have blamed a million different things for ruining their lives — but seldom if ever have they blamed prayer.

On the other hand, an awful lot of people have said they've really found their lives through prayer.

If you don't pray much, give it a shot. Try ten minutes a day. Five in the morning, five at night. You can start with some memorized prayers if that's how you feel comfortable. They're fine. But really keep your mind tuned in to the words. Then work in some absolute, gut-level, letting-it-all-spill-out communication. And leave time for listening.

Ten minutes a day to start. It works out to .69444 percent of your time. You had that much time to spare, remember?

9. Don't Fall for an Old Junquer

"Good evening! And welcome once again to *Conversational Junque,* America's newest, most exciting interview and talk show! I'm Harvey Verbose, your host, with another fascinating lineup of guests, and it's time to meet them.

"To my right is Sandi Jones. Sandi is currently a student at the Metropolitan University of Medicine and hopes to become a doctor. Sandi, give us a quick description of your classes at Metro Med."

"That's hard to do, Harvey. I cut most of the classes."

"You cut classes in med school?"

"Yeah. They're pretty boring. All about bones and blood and organs and stuff. I don't get anything out of them."

"But you want to be a doctor someday, don't you?"

"Oh sure. Doctors make a bundle. I figure I'll get there somehow or other."

"Thanks for a . . . really different outlook on medicine, Sandi. Our next guest is Luke Brown. Luke, I understand you used to be very active in politics, but that's changed. True?"

"Yeah. I never get into that stuff anymore."

"Why not, Luke?"

"It's so phony. I know people who spend time on campaigns for somebody or other, but they're really just doing it because of their friends. They don't believe that much in the candidate. And some of the politicians too — they're just in it for the publicity and the bucks."

"All of them — all the time?"

"No, but some of them some of the time. Turns me off."

"So you've quit completely?"

"You got it. Who needs to hang around with a bunch of hypocrites?"

"Okay, Luke. We'll get back to you. In the meantime, here's Bud Morgan, and Bud is into soccer, right?"

"Yeah. Soccer's pretty cool."

"What team do you play for, Bud?"

"Oh, I don't play for a team. I couldn't hack going to practices and all

27

those games. I mean, some of 'em are scheduled *before noon,* man! I can't get up that early on a weekend. The games last too long anyway.''

"So . . . you don't really play soccer.''

"Well, I don't play on a team in a game with other people. I do it my way. I sort of lie on the couch and *think* about kicking the ball and all that stuff.''

"That's soccer?''

"Sure. If it's soccer for me, then it's soccer. Who's to say what's soccer and what isn't? It's all just somebody's opinion anyway, so I've got my own opinion.''

"It's a real different evening here, folks. Let's check with our last guest. This is Mary Clark, and Mary says she's interested in making the world a better place, right?''

"That's it exactly, Harvey. I just think it would be a real sweet thing to do, you know?''

"I think so too, Mary. Tell us something of your plans for the future — some things you'd like to do to make the world better.''

"Oh, I don't plan on *doing* much. You don't need to make a big deal out of doing things. What's important is that you're nice and you don't hurt people.''

"Well, that's a great start. But that's it? Just be nice and don't hurt people?''

"Yuh-huh. And help people.''

"How?''

"I dunno. Just, you know, be helpful.''

Have you ever heard stuff like that before? Probably. It just centers around a slightly different topic. It goes like this:

"Church? Religion? It's boring. I don't get anything out of it. I still believe in God, and I want to get to heaven and all, but . . . well, I'll make it somehow or other.''

"Why go to church when it's so phony? I know people who never miss a Sunday, and then during the week they do all kinds of wrong stuff. At least I don't pretend to be holy.''

"I can't get into all that regular church stuff, see. Lasts too long, for one thing, and I don't think you have to get together with other people or have any formal rules or stuff like that. I just do it whatever way I feel like.''

"All that matters is that you don't hurt people. You don't have to believe anything special, or go to church, or keep any rules. Just, like, you know, be nice.''

Make sense?

About as much as the guests on *Conversational Junque.*

SECTION FOUR:

GETTING THERE

10. The Road Map: Don't Leave Home Without It

Your coach has called a special meeting. The gossip is that a special, dynamic, no-fail new strategy for winning is about to be announced. So you can't wait for the coach's speech. Here it is:

"Next game go out there and play like crazy, okay? Score a lot. And don't let the other team score. Got it? That's it, team. Dismissed."

"Huh? That's *it*? Hey, Coach, you want to give us just a little hint on *how* we do this? Like, what exactly do we *do*?"

It's the first day of class. You're listening to your history teacher. You'd like to get an idea of what's expected in this class. Here it comes:

"Good morning, class. Now I want all of you to study history as hard as you can and learn lots about what happened in the past. I'll be back at the end of the semester and give you a test. Good luck and remember to study hard."

Huh? History of what? From when to when? What kind of a test? How about a little more information?

You flip the TV dial to the famous TV chef's program.

"Here's how to make this delicious, nutritious casserole that everyone will go wild over. Use only the right ingredients, no others. And don't bake it too long. On the other hand, don't bake it too little, either. See how easy? Just follow those directions and you can't go wrong."

Oh really? You call those things directions?

General goals or ideas are fine. You need them. But you're lost without particular guidelines. An Eskimo who wants to visit Disney World needs more than the advice, "Head south."

That's the reason for the Commandments.

Sometimes, unfortunately, the word *commandments* gives people a negative feeling: "Stuff I gotta do and even more stuff I'm not allowed to do. Gotta play it straight or I'll get busted when I die."

But without God's commandments, you'd be as lost as the people in the examples above — the players who were told only to score a lot, the students who were told only to study a lot, and the TV audience who were told only to use the right ingredients and correct baking time. If you were in each of those situations, you'd be grateful for very definite guidelines or rules. Rules show you the *way* to do it right so you end up where you want to be.

That's how the Israelites looked upon the laws God gave them. They called their collection of laws "Torah." They showed the way. The way to God. The way to be what they were supposed to be.

A map, for example, shows the way to get somewhere, and it's a very welcome thing to have. That's how the Israelites looked upon their laws. They thanked God for giving those laws much the same as you would thank someone who gave you a detailed map to a destination you wanted to reach. His laws were among his gifts.

A strange way of looking at laws?

Not really. Not if you really want to get to where they lead you.

11. Passing Isn't Automatic

Ignatius Horatio McGillicuddy just got a 63 percent on a biology test. (Actually, the character could be called Melissa Jones or Bob Smith or Ann Jackson. He/she stands for you, me — anybody.)

Anyway, that 63 percent was bad news. Then came a 74 percent on a Spanish test. Not a complete disaster, but not good news either. Then came the 51 percent on the English exam. Academic wipeout.

There are several things Iggy can do about this state of affairs.

1. He can spend hours moping around, feeling rotten, and telling himself that he's nothing but a big zero — a hopeless, worthless academic slob. This is not very healthy.

2. He can dismiss the whole thing with "So what?" "Who cares?" and "Big deal." He can say his 51 percent isn't really so bad because one other guy got a 48 percent. This is likewise not an intelligent reaction. Both this and the first one are escape devices. They're designed to avoid a confrontation with responsibility.

3. He can just plain not even look at the grades when any future tests are returned. Instead he can crumple them up and use them to practice jump shots at the wastebasket without looking to see whether there was a 93 or a 39 at the top of the paper. This is like strolling toward the end of the diving board without bothering to check whether there's water in the pool or not.

These three reactions are very different from each other, but they also have something in common. They all avoid what's real. Whenever you try to avoid what's real, sooner or later you hit a brick wall.

Consider another way of failing a test or challenge — the challenge to do what's right, to act as Christians should. That's called sin, and sin is real. It's real, and it's also an unpleasant idea. You'd rather think about pizza and yesterday's game and next week's concert.

Gardeners, of course, would rather think about prize-winning roses than weeds, and quarterbacks would rather recall touchdown passes than interceptions and fumbles. But you can't just tune those things out. Weeds and fumbles are real. Sin is real.

As seen in the opening example, you can have three *unrealistic* reactions to sin.

One is to put yourself down as a moral slob who seldom does anything right. It's possible for you to go overboard with guilt and expect to be perfect before you allow God's love to touch you.

A second wrong reaction is to dull your conscience so much that sin seems about the same as breathing. No big deal, part of life, everybody does it, no way around it. Then you get to a point where nothing seems really sinful except perhaps cold-blooded mass murder.

Third, you can take an "I don't care" attitude — literally not care whether you've done right or wrong, whether you've headed down a path of increasing sinfulness or not.

All of these avoid what's real. And you just can't afford to do that.

Some people don't like to admit to sin in their lives because they're turned off by the idea of human creatures pleading before an angry God, confessing over and over how awful they are. But God never painted that picture at all. Jesus told his apostles, "I call you friends," even though they weren't a group of saints with 14-carat halos at the time. (One of them denied him three times just a couple of hours later, and most of the others deserted him.)

Does that mean God just ignores sin — and you can, too? No. The only people Jesus got really upset with were people who either thought they were too good to be sinful or didn't care one way or another. But the people who knew they had sinned and were sorry and wanted another shot — to them he showed understanding and forgiveness and love like the world had never seen.

You need that "examination of conscience." Not simply to conclude how awful you are but to find where you have gone wrong so that you can improve. The great baseball pitcher Dizzy Dean said, "When you stop getting better, you stop being good." That can be true of living life in general, not just throwing a baseball. Professional sports teams and even individual players watch game films to identify and correct mistakes, to revise and improve. You need to view the game film of your life every now and then. Otherwise you'll never change.

Sin is real. It won't just evaporate from your life by itself, either. And you can't afford to be unrealistic about that.

12. Conscience: License to Drive a Human Life

Driving is fun for most people. If you drive (or you're learning to drive), you probably enjoy it. Now and then maybe you wish that there were no such things as speed limits and lanes. No stop signs or yield signs or traffic lights. Seems like it would be a real trip to do absolutely anything you wanted with the car.

Imagine this: Nothing around but miles upon square miles of concrete in every direction. No lane markers, no speed limits, no signals, no rules of any kind. Just you and your car and lots of empty space just waiting for you to get behind the wheel and do whatever seems like a kick.

For a while there would be a thrill to it, no question. But you'd have to admit a couple other things, too.

First, it would get boring. Yeah, for real — boring. Not ever going anywhere eventually gets to be a drag, even when you're not going anywhere at high speed. And besides going nowhere, you'd be proving nothing while you're doing it. With no lanes to stay inside of, no situations to handle, no places to arrive at, there would be little or no challenge. All you'd demonstrate is that you know how to step on the gas pedal. Wow. Heavy talent.

So, sooner or later would come the temptation to do a little slalom, some fishtailing, a few spins, and then some even riskier ones. Even with no other objects or obstacles in sight, there would be a decent chance of wipeout . . . wheels up in the air instead of on the concrete.

Operating a human life without a conscience, without any regard for right or wrong, is something like that. What seems like unlimited freedom eventually leaves people burned out.

But a place with nothing but empty concrete doesn't exist. To make the example real, put some other cars on that empty surface — and some homes and lots of people. That's real life. Then imagine somebody still driving as though there were nothing else around, as though speed limits and signals and traffic laws didn't exist — just put the pedal to the floor and have kicks.

Lots of people are going to get hurt. Including, eventually, the driver.

That's what people are like when they go through life without listening to a well-formed conscience. They become destroyers — of people in their paths and eventually of themselves. Often, they're hardly aware of how many people they hurt with their, "Who cares if it's wrong?" approach to life.

That's not the kind of life you want for yourself. Christians are builders, not destroyers. You simply can't ignore conscience and call yourself Christian — or even human.

But conscience isn't a little box implanted into your brain at birth which automatically beeps or buzzes or burps when you do something wrong or think of doing it. Conscience is simply your ability to make judgments about actions. Call it a mental muscle that operates in the area of right and wrong.

Like any other ability, you can simply refuse to use and develop it. You can let it get flabby just like a muscle that you seldom use. Or you can twist and warp it in the wrong direction until it has huge blind spots, or until it spits out wild, off-base, sick judgments about right and wrong.

How often do you read in the newspapers about people doing really horrible things — without seeing anything really wrong in them? Those people didn't begin that way. Most of them did some convenient conscience twisting or neglecting along the way, usually a little at a time, until even gruesome things didn't seem so terribly wrong.

Since conscience is an ability you have, you're responsible for developing it and keeping it in good shape. You're responsible for gathering correct information so that you can make good judgments.

In some ways, it's like a watch. To tell the correct time (and arrange your life accordingly), you look at your watch. But you can't just spin the hands on your watch to whatever time you'd *like* it to be and then say, "This must be the right time because that's what my watch says." Time isn't whatever you want it to be. Time isn't whatever your watch indicates. There *is* such a thing as the *real, correct time*.

There *is* such a thing as a real right and wrong, and a correct conscience puts you in tune with it. Right and wrong aren't just what you want them to be, any more than the correct time is whatever hour you make your watch indicate. Both your watch and your conscience guide you correctly when you set them correctly.

A little kid might get a silly kick out of saying, "I'm gonna decide what time it is and go by that. I'm not gonna listen to anybody else or look at anybody's watch. I'll have my own time." You laugh because it's just a little kid acting silly.

In a way, it's similar when a person decides, "I'm going to make up my

35

own ideas about right and wrong, whatever I want them to be, and go by that.'' But it's not just silly or laughable anymore. This is more than a kid who might miss his or her school bus. This is a person turning his or her life into a weapon that can do a lot of damage to other people.

Where do you go for the correct information? Jesus said a lot about how to live. It's in the New Testament. He also left behind a group to carry on and interpret what he began — his Church. ''Whoever hears you, hears me,'' he told the apostles.

Chemists and astronomers, doctors and mechanics, governors and carpenters and investors . . . none of them tunes out what people in their fields before them have discovered. Christians who need to decide about right and wrong shouldn't either.

SECTION FIVE:

DECIDE, RIGHT? YEAH — AND DECIDE *RIGHT*

13. Elvira's Catsupy Apple Pie

Elvira McSnurg stood at her kitchen counter, tense and trembling. Her hand was wrapped around the forbidden bottle of catsup.

"Don't do it!" a voice within her whispered. "It's against everything you ever learned in the *Better Homes and Gardens Cookbook!*"

She glanced at the oven dial. She had already set it for four hundred and eighty degrees. *"No!"* the voice within her commanded again. "Don't pour that catsup on top of that apple pie and bake it at four hundred and eighty degrees! It's not the way a good apple pie should be made!"

Elvira *knew* that. She had made many apple pies — correctly. Never before had she been tempted to cover the apple pie with a half inch of catsup and bake it at four hundred and eighty degrees.

And yet . . . and yet maybe this time it wouldn't be so wrong. Maybe this time it would actually be the right thing to do, she tried to tell herself. Harvey loved apple pie with catsup topping burnt to a crisp. He had told her so just yesterday with a gleam in his eye. And today he was coming to dinner.

Harvey . . . dear, dear Harvey. At first he had been her editor at the newspaper. He was still that, but now he was her boyfriend, too. She needed the job. She needed companionship. She liked Harvey.

Should she risk it all by baking a regular apple pie instead of an apple pie covered with catsup burnt to a crisp?

What will Elvira do? No one knows. The story isn't finished yet. But her present situation is meant to illustrate a point.

Here's her problem: She knows the right way to make a good apple pie. But some other items have entered the picture. There's her job (Harvey as boss) and there's romance (Harvey as boyfriend). Both are important to her. The result is a *conflict;* she faces a challenge to her knowledge and experience of baking apple pies the right way.

So what's wrong with baking a weird apple pie the way Harvey likes it and keeping both her job and her romance? Nothing. What is done to an apple pie might make it delicious or make it putrid, but neither one is a matter of good versus evil.

But what if Harvey wants something besides a gross apple pie? What if he wants Elvira to fix up some payroll records to hide a few thousand dollars he stole? What if he wants her to type an article full of lies about an innocent person? What if he wants some casual sex after office hours?

Then it becomes a *moral* conflict. Elvira's dilemma demonstrates the ingredients that make up the conflict. (1) The "I know" part: I know or am rather sure that a certain action is wrong. (2) The "I want" part: Doing what I know is wrong will get me something I want. I want it because it seems to fill certain needs I have.

In many cases, the "I want" not only seems attractive, it starts to look OK — maybe even admirable! I don't say, "This is a horribly gross, disgustingly evil thing to do — therefore, I will do it" when I make wrong moral choices. Usually I convince myself that the evil choice isn't really all that wrong — maybe not wrong at all.

That's called rationalizing. The "I want" part of me says, "Okay, generally this is probably the wrong thing to do; but in this case, for me, it's not really wrong because I have good reasons for acting this way; and in the long run, good things will probably come from it; and besides, it's the only choice there really is; and on top of that, I have such strong feelings I can't help myself and jabberjabberwockywockyandsoforth."

The "I know" part of me comes back with, "Don't feed yourself all that sweetened garbage. It's still garbage. Wrong is wrong."

The "I want" takes over and says, "Okay, wellyeahbutinaway. . . . "

That's a moral conflict, and often it's tough to work through something like that. It *is* true that individual circumstances can make a difference in the rightness or wrongness of an action. But many times, arguing that "my circumstances change everything" is just an easy cop out.

One of the biggest dangers you face in a moral conflict is burying your head in the sand and pretending there *isn't* any conflict. That's tempting to do.

But would you let yourself be convinced that apple pie with a topping of burnt catsup is a normal, OK apple pie . . . or that there's no such thing as a right and a wrong way to make an apple pie?

Don't let yourself be convinced that there's no such thing as a real moral decision, either.

14. "I Didn't Know the Gun Was Loaded"

Those words are not much comfort if you're on the receiving end of a load of buckshot. It's not much comfort if you're the one who pulled the trigger, either. There are consequences to pulling triggers.

But strangely, there are some "guns" that people prefer to ignore. They'd rather stay in the dark and not find out the way things really are — just in case they don't like it.

For example, some people have nagging pains in their gut, but they put off going to the doctor. They're afraid the doctor might run some tests and come up with serious, unpleasant news. So they avoid the doctor and just hope the pain and the problem will go away by itself.

In a way that's understandable; but it's also not too smart. When it comes to something as serious as your health, you need to know exactly what the situation is. If eating tomatoes will kill you in two months, you need to know that so you can stop eating them, no matter how good tomatoes may taste to you.

It's important to know the truth about things that affect your *moral* health, too — things that involve right and wrong and how to live a life "worthy of the calling you have received," as Saint Paul wrote to the Ephesians (4:1).

Not all choices between right and wrong are completely crystal clear. Besides, you *grow* in your understanding of right and wrong just as you grow in many other ways. Because of that, it's sometimes tempting to "stay dumb" and deliberately not try to find the answer.

People often ask, "Is it wrong to do something if you don't know it's wrong?"

If the situation is as simple as that question is on the surface, the answer is also simple: "No." Pure and simple.

For instance, if a three-year-old takes a piece of candy from the grocery store shelf because he or she simply thinks it's there for people to enjoy, the child wouldn't be stealing. Sure, technically the action is not right, but the child didn't know that. Nobody in his or her right mind is going to say the kid sinned.

But there are few situations like that. You almost never have zero percent knowledge that something should or should not be done. You often have a pretty decent idea that an action leans toward right or toward wrong, even if you don't have it a hundred percent figured out, proven, and locked up.

But what if you're really not sure?

If it's not a decision that has to be made in the next few minutes, it's a smart idea to ask someone who can help sort it out. That doesn't mean someone who will give you the easiest answer, the one you may be hoping to hear. Going to a successful bank robber and asking, "What's your opinion about borrowing from banks without their permission?" is not an honest attempt to learn what's right and wrong.

Intelligent people frequently ask other people's advice. Even Einstein studied scientists before him. You can make good decisions only after you have all the necessary information. That holds true in most things from business investments to moral situations.

Pray for the insight to know what the right decision is and for the courage to follow it. Really pray. (Don't cop out with "Oh God, if robbing this bank is wrong, send down a lightning bolt to stop me from doing it.")

Search and talk and pray and then act according to your conscience. You can't be faulted if you've done that.

15. So Many Ways to Go

Announcer: And now we return to *As the Months of Our Lives Turn Over and Over,* the continuing drama of ordinary people who have more problems than they have blood cells.

Samantha-Jane: I want to thank all of you for coming to try to help me. I just . . . I can't decide. There's Larry. There's Darrell. There's Keith. And faithful old Mergatroyd. I could marry any of them — but which one? *Which one?* I can't take it! The confusion is killing me! It's worse than having hair that won't bounce and bathroom tile that doesn't shine and washed dishes that don't turn out virtually spotless!

Kelly: Samantha-Jane, Larry's the only guy you even need to think about. He's cute, he's rich, he's every girl's dream. It's the only *right* choice.

Howard: Sam, as your practically all-knowing brother, I have to be candid about this and tell it like it is. For all-around dependability, you gotta go with Keith. Listen, Sam, I know the guy personally. He's awesome. And he's *right* for you.

Marie: Samantha-Jane, Howard means well, but what does he know? Now look at Darrell — just *look.* Now there is a hunk! Besides, you're a Gemini and he's a Pisces. That proves it. You're *right* for each other.

Jeannie: Follow your feelings, Samantha-Jane. Trust your heart. Listen to the deepest stirrings within you. They'll lead you to Mergatroyd, Sam. He's captain of the ping-pong team, and his picture is on a cornflake box. In your heart, you know he's *right.*

Now, before you get sinus heartburn and need a maximum strength, anti-garbage capsule, stop and think for a moment.

Samantha-Jane has a problem. She doesn't know which guy is the right guy. Notice she has many people telling her different things about which choice is right. She illustrates a common situation. Different ideas come from different people about many things — including right and wrong.

Example: "Is it OK to get really buzzed?"

"Never. Anytime you put yourself under the influence of alcohol, you're committing serious sin."

"Is it OK? You serious? What a dumb question. Of course, it's OK. It's the most normal thing in the world. Everybody does it."

"Well, maybe it's OK once in a while, but you shouldn't get in the habit of it. If you do, that's wrong."

"It's wrong unless you have a really good reason, like something terrible just happened and you need to forget, or something great just happened and you want to celebrate."

See?

If Samantha-Jane were real, here are two things that you can be pretty sure would *not* happen: (1) She would not decide that it's permanently impossible to choose and therefore go off to live alone on a desert island. (2) She would not decide that it doesn't make any difference which guy she chooses anyway and just pick a name out of a box. It's too important to leave to chance; somehow or other, she will make a decision.

You need to use decision-making powers when you hear conflicting things about right and wrong. It's tempting to think, "With so many opinions, there's no way of telling what's right," or "It probably doesn't make any real difference anyway."

It's tempting because it's convenient. If you figure you can never find the answer to what's right or that there is no real answer, you seem to be off the hook and free to do whatever is easiest or whatever turns you on at the moment.

Avoiding the issue is probably the most common way to "chicken out" in the area of moral decisions. But it's like saying, "There are so many rules in this driving manual; I'll never remember them all. So I'll just go out and drive. Nobody can blame me for breaking rules I don't know." That doesn't make much sense.

Sorting right from wrong may take effort, but coming to an honorable conclusion is not impossible. If *you* matter, then so does how you live your life.

16. And Just Who Said So?

I have this huge stack of English papers to correct: Stories for Creative Writing. Want to look over a few?

"at 3:27 pm the oven timmer buzzed in elaine Stantons kitchen, a few seconds latter the doorbell rang, if the order had been reversed she might of lived. But by 3:29 she was dead."

That's Missy's paper. As an opening for a murder mystery, it's positively terrific. Unfortunately, a few little items like spelling, punctuation, and usage came out the opposite of terrific. If I use pure *creativity* as a standard to grade that paragraph, it gets an A. If I go by *correctness* . . . well, let's move on.

"With the quick, deft movements born of vast experience in the domestic arts, Aunt Sandra reached into the sink and lifted up a gleaming plate, still swirly with soapy water; she held it beneath the stream of clean water from the faucet, tilted it to rinse each side, and placed it gently in its proper place in the dish strainer."

That's Lori's paper. What a sentence! It's more than correct: It flows, it's balanced, it's grammatically gorgeous. Unfortunately, who wants to read about Aunt Sandra doing dishes? If I judge by correctness and sentence style, there's an A for sure. If I judge by creativity in choice of subject . . . well, let's move on again. Here's Todd's story.

"The sergeant got up from his seat by all the knobs and buttons and went to the back part of the helicopter. . . . " The story goes on for twenty-three pages. It's about terrorists hijacking an Army helicopter.

However, Todd has never been in the Army or in a helicopter, and he hasn't hung around with terrorists or even read much about them. So the story doesn't sound very realistic. Plus, the spelling, punctuation, and grammar are sloppy. Still, twenty-three pages is admirable; I only required four. If I grade pure effort and quantity, another A. If I grade the quality of the results, that's a different story.

Some experts on teaching say creativity is the most important item, practically the only one. Others say no, basic correctness comes first.

Still others advise giving most credit to a student's effort. There are even some who advise letting students grade each other's papers.

All these influences are working on me when I sit down to grade a set of papers. To do a good job, I have to decide something ahead of time: *What standards am I going to use?* And I'd better use the same standards on the last paper in the stack that I used on the first.

When you face right/wrong decisions, many influences are at work on you, too.

For obvious starters, parents. To parents, add other adults: relatives, coaches, teachers, neighbors. Then add classmates and friends, the people you call "peers," who make up a very powerful group which influences your decisions.

Which voices do you remember most when you're faced with a right/wrong decision?

Besides these, which are easy enough to see, there are other voices aiming messages at you: TV shows, movies, books, magazines, newspaper articles, song lyrics, advertisements. True, they're not directly involved in the advice-giving business, and they don't usually talk with you in person. But they're a bigger influence on some people than parents, friends, and other people who *do* talk in person.

How many young people decide it's OK to get stoned or to sleep around because one of their favorite rock stars does it or sings about it or both? How many people decide it's OK to cheat when a well-known city official misuses city funds and gets caught purely by accident? These influences are harder to recognize, but they're there. Count on it.

But you're not brainless sponges that have to soak up everything around you. You're not meant to be wimpy little carbon copies of somebody else. You're individuals, meant to make your own decisions based on good standards that you've thought about and made your own.

Not that your standards of acting will be unlike anything anybody else has ever thought of — first time ever on planet Earth. That's impossible.

Hopefully there will be lots of similarities between the guidelines you decide to follow and the guidelines for living that Jesus gave to the world. For example, they're a much safer investment than the advice for living which your friendly neighborhood Joe Cool gives you.

Jesus will be around for quite a while, and he'll be a part of your life, if not now, very definitely at the end of it. Your Joe Cool classmate may not even be in your life at all two years from now.

17. The Great Supermarket Showdown

You've seen this scene. It's repeated daily at supermarkets throughout the nation. Characters: Kid (perhaps three to ten years old) and Parent (older).

Parent and Kid approach checkout lane. Kid wants candy, grabs a bar or bag or box and puts it in shopping cart. Parent explains that Kid already has had enough candy and they're not going to buy more. Parent puts candy back on shelf.

Kid re-grabs candy, tosses it back in cart with great foot stomping, arm waving, and fake crying. Parent tells Kid to stop. Kid does not stop. Parent finally says, "Well, just *one,* but you can't eat it now. You'll have to wait till after supper."

Kid instantly recovers from tears and rips open candy wrapper. Parent pretends to give profound attention to unloading grocery cart and thus not notice Kid pigging out.

You have to feel sorry for the kid. He or she is learning a disastrous lesson at the hands of a wimpy parent: "If I want something, I just act like a brat, break a few rules, and sooner or later I'll get it, even if it's something I shouldn't have."

Sometimes that lesson sticks around and becomes a regular way of looking at life — long after Kid is no longer a kid. At sixteen or eighteen or twenty-five, he or she won't jump up and down, scream, cry, and wave arms. The methods will change, but the attitude doesn't.

"I want — therefore I will get, no matter what." It's easy to see that this is immature and harmful in a five-year-old. You can easily agree that parents can't afford to let their kids start thinking that way.

But it's harder to see the same truth when you're thinking about yourself. You're not five years old anymore. And growing up brings with it the responsibility of deciding things for yourselves. So you might think that anybody's "no" — even God's — is an unfair restriction of your free choice, a denial of your maturity. "I'm not a little kid anymore, so I should be able to do what I want."

Does following a code of right and wrong really limit your freedom?

The answer is a big "yes" — *if* freedom means doing absolutely anything that seems like a trick. But that's not what it really means.

Besides, you can get trapped in that kind of "freedom." Here's Joe Free and Cool — he's seventeen. For a couple of years he's been very well acquainted with booze and grass. No one is going to tell him what to do, no way. He runs his own life, man.

So he tries to handle school and getting regularly high at the same time. This means scrambling to cover for cut classes, scrambling to copy homework at the last minute, walking into tests he doesn't know anything about and hoping he can cheat enough to pass (without getting busted). It means constantly hiding the evidence, lying about where he's been, lifting a little money here and there to cover bottle and joint costs, and always wondering whether he's covered his tracks well enough.

That's freedom?

If every time I see something attractive, the spoiled little kid inside me starts screaming "I want!" and won't shut up until I figure out a way to get it (legally or illegally), *is that being free?*

Real freedom helps you grow and it brings you peace. It doesn't give you a quick thrill and then make you pay for it later. Real freedom doesn't open a small door and then slam the big ones shut in your face. Moral codes offer guidance not to limit your freedom but to keep you going in the right direction.

Toward God.

SECTION SIX:
QUICK THRILLS
AND CRASH
LANDINGS

18. The Quick Thrill

"NOW!!! DON'T PUT IT OFF!!! GET IT NOW!!! DON'T WAIT!!! YOU NEED IT NOW!!! YOU DESERVE IT NOW!!! BUY IT NOW — ENJOY IT TODAY!!!"

How often have you heard that message? Very. It's in every advertisement you've ever seen and every commercial you've ever heard. (Have you ever seen a commercial that said, "After you've saved enough money, consider buying our product?" Of course not.)

Even the products that you're supposed to buy right now go into action almost instantly.

"Get beautiful, shiny, bouncy hair in five minutes with Queen Konga Deep Conditioning Creme Rinse!"

"Get a Super-Hunk Body in just ten minutes a day with the new Maxi-Aerobic, Ultra-Psychometric, Multi-Cycle Exerciser!"

"Watch your family go wild over dessert with new Instant Sugary Goop! Just toss it in a bowl with some milk and let it chill for three minutes!"

All this tends to limit your vision to the next few minutes, or at least the next few hours or days, and that's an awfully shortsighted vision. Sure, you should enjoy the present moment. But never thinking beyond the next few minutes or the next couple of days is dangerous. It often backfires, and, more important, it can lead you in wrong directions: "Just this once — I need to feel good . . . *now.*"

After a couple dozen times of "Just this once because I need it *now,*" you're set in a direction, but it's the wrong one.

So it's important to check your direction from time to time and ask, "If I keep on doing the same things I'm doing now, keep making the same kinds of decisions . . . how will I turn out? Where will I be next year . . . five years from now?"

Think of it as a pilot guiding an airplane's flight. If the plane goes a couple degrees off course, that may not seem like a disaster; this can easily enough be corrected if it's caught quickly. But the longer the plane travels off course, the farther away it gets from the intended final destination.

That's not a perfect example of your relationship with God, but it can help you think about a part of it.

See, very few people decide all at once that they're going to hang up this religion business for good . . . that faith is a lot of nonsense . . . that God is a big zero in their lives. Almost nobody does that. But lots of people drift away from God gradually, a degree at a time, often without thinking about it.

Then one day they do think about it and realize how far away they seem to have come. But by then, unfortunately, they may not care any longer. Or they may give up because going back seems too far, too difficult.

You can't see into the future. But it's very smart to try to predict what your future will be like if you continue your present course.

Particularly if you're in the habit of quick thrills of any kind. They add up and become a general direction. You need to check and see whether you really want to head there.

19. High Stakes in the High Random Rodeo

Imagine your ultimate set of wheels . . . the vehicle of your dreams. A Rolls Royce or a BMW. A prize-winning competition van. A collector's classic like a '57 Chevy or a '66 Mustang.

Whatever it is for you, imagine everything about it as vividly as you can. See the gleaming paint, feel the interior's leather and crushed velvet. Listen to the incredible sound system. Imagine every gadget, every extra luxury ever invented.

It's one of a kind. And imagine you got it *free* from someone who loves you. A showcase, a masterpiece of design and performance . . . free!

Now imagine something else. One day you're approached by a guy who tells you it would be a real trip to enter your automotive masterpiece in a "High Random Rodeo."

You don't know what that is, so you ask.

He explains that in a High Random Rodeo, people bring their cars to this huge, almost empty parking lot. But they don't drive the cars themselves. A tiny computer is installed in each car. The computer "drives" the car according to a random, unpredictable pattern.

In the process, of course, cars occasionally flip over while turning too fast. Transmissions get ripped apart from being shifted into reverse at high speeds. The cars sometimes smash into each other and some get totaled. But that's all part of the show.

You ask if people get hurt as well as the cars.

He admits that once in a while the computer inside one of the cars goes really crazy and the car hits somebody. But it doesn't happen *that* often, he explains, and the risk is worth it because everybody is having such a good time. Besides, bad things don't *have* to happen. Several guys, he says, have been bringing their cars to the rodeo regularly, and so far there doesn't seem to be any serious, permanent damage.

You figure there must be incredible prizes for taking chances like that with your car. But there aren't.

"There's no prize — it's just fun to do, man. And all the people there are cool people. You come to the rodeo, you're cool, okay?"

Your opinion, please.

When this situation is proposed, most kids say, "That would be really stupid." And many go on to say, "It's just plain wrong, too."

It *is* wrong simply to waste something valuable or take the risk of wasting it for no reason. It's an insult to the person who gave the gift. And when lives as well as machinery are being risked, that makes it even more wrong. Most people would never risk putting their cars out of control like that. You probably wouldn't either.

Please think at least as much of your body and your mind. Because you'll probably be asked — you've probably been asked already — to put them out of control with chemicals.

Your bodies, your minds, your lives, are worth a billion billion times more than the most elaborate set of wheels anybody will ever design. They're priceless gifts you received absolutely free from God. Is it OK to put them out of control with a chemical?

Think about that question, too. Because when somebody asks you to get into the rodeo, you need to know what you're going to say.

20. The Booze Blues

This chapter is about those other people — those other kids, the ones who get to be statistics and get written up in newspapers.

It's so easy to think that way: Other kids become alcoholics. Other people get killed or kill somebody else because they drove drunk . . . or even half drunk . . . or even a little buzzed. (You don't have to be blacked out in order to misjudge distance or angles or speed or time.)

"So a lot of kids get polluted now and then — so what? Doesn't everybody get a good buzz on once in a while? Anyway, it doesn't have anything to do with me. It won't mess up my life."

Mistake.

Maybe this attitude is a way of defending yourselves from what you really know: Alcohol is dangerous. So you pretend that it could hurt only other people.

Or maybe you've heard the anti-booze and drug story so often that you tune it out. You get tired of hearing the statistics. Besides, you listen to a recovered alcoholic or druggie and you think, "See, even if you do get into it too heavy, you just check yourself into a rehab program and get straightened out. There's always a way back."

Mistake.

If you think alcohol could never mess up your life, you already have something in common with most alcoholics. And the scary statistics aren't invented by little old ladies who want to keep you from letting loose and having fun. Those scary statistics are just plain true. They happened to people just like you . . . people who never thought it would happen to them.

The recovered alcoholics and former druggies who come to talk at your school *are the exceptions. Most teenage alcoholics and druggies don't make it back — they just don't.*

"But it's my life. If I *want* to take a chance on messing it up, that's my business. Maybe I think getting buzzed or stoned is worth the risk — that's my business."

Mistake.

A bombed, stoned, burned-out life is never only that one person's business. Never.

Money for the stuff has to come from somewhere. Weekly allowances and part-time jobs hardly pay enough to support a beginning habit, much less a heavy one. So the user either steals the money — from another person — or gets it from dealing drugs to mess up still more lives.

What about the family whose lives are upset, maybe even torn apart, by the user's habit? Aren't *they* involved?

Like most other people, drinkers and users get married and have kids. What about the kids who get a lousy start in life because Mom and/or Dad drinks or smokes or snorts or sniffs or shoots up? Aren't *they* involved?

What about the people who end up dead or crippled because a user decided to take a little trip in a car along with the chemical trip he or she was already taking? Aren't *they* involved?

Put one drinker or druggie in a group of ten straights and he or she will instantly begin to recruit. (*"C'mon, man — be cool!"*) What about the two or three or more who end up hooked? Aren't *they* involved?

"It's *my* life, man — so it's my business and nobody else's."

What a really bad joke.

SECTION SEVEN:

THE (SHHH!) YOU-KNOW-WHAT PART

21. Warning: No Parent Admitted Without Mature Kid

Warning! Warning! Red alert! Security factor ten! We are about to discuss . . . *you-know-what!* OK, I guess we'll actually have to use the word. *Sex.* (Sorry. Didn't mean to shock you; some things have to be, you know?)

Here are the rules: Sex will be discussed only in hushed whispers. You must keep your eyes down and not look at each other. No one, of course, is allowed to laugh. Above all, *try not to be too interested.* In fact, try to be at least a little bored.

Dumb, right? But there was a time when some folks approached sexuality that way. That happened because of a false idea: Real sexuality and real Christian holiness don't mix too well; if you want to be really, genuinely holy, don't experience sexuality, don't talk about it, don't think about it — in fact, try to be turned off by the whole idea.

That idea was bad news then and it still is now. Here's why — and it's a reason we still keep on forgetting.

God invented sex. Not Hollywood. Not *Playboy.* Not *General Hospital.* Not Dr. Ruth or the local sex expert among your classmates. God.

So where did people get the idea that sex maybe isn't so nice? Certainly not from God. For one thing, God is not an idiot or a madman — he would not create something deep within you and then turn around and say, "By the way, this is really kind of gross, so try to stay away from it." And sexuality is spread all through his message to you in the Bible. Obviously God doesn't think you should half hide this part of human nature.

The idea that sex isn't too nice can also come from the realization that *what some people do with their sexuality* isn't so great. Some people turn themselves into selfish, sexually consuming monsters who regard other people as sexual objects to be used. They hurt, sometimes even destroy, those other people, and they don't really care as long as their own nerve endings feel good. But even all that doesn't make sex itself a little bit dirty.

In fact, it proves the opposite. Think of all the sin and suffering and garbage that wouldn't happen if there were no such thing as sex. Rape, prostitution, pornography, child molesting, abortion, murder (people kill over sex), unwanted and neglected kids . . . you can extend the list until you get sick to your stomach.

None of it would happen if sex didn't exist. And God knew this from the beginning.

He created sex anyway.

What does that tell you? One of two things. Either God is a raving idiot or *there's something so beautiful, so good about sex when it goes right that it's worth the risk of all the things that can go wrong.*

Let's start by dropping the silly, "Baby, I know it A-L-L-L" act. One of the neat things about life as God planned it is that it's a learning experience, including learning about sexuality. But lots of people act as though they already know it all, even at eleven or twelve years old. They'll admit they have lots to learn about almost anything else: math, history, swimming, auto mechanics, almost anything but sex. When it comes to sex, "There's nothing you can tell me that I haven't known for ages, man — I mean, I've been around, you know?" They're the local sex experts in any class or group or neighborhood. While other kids played with blocks in their playpens at age two, these kids were sitting in their playpens writing sex manuals. Well, that's what they'd like you to think.

Besides, simply knowing the differences in male and female plumbing and simply knowing the mechanics of reproduction is miles away from appreciating sexuality. It's like knowing that in baseball a person swings a bat, hits the ball, and runs around the field. True? Well, yes — but is that the whole story? Not quite. Neither is simply knowing the mechanics of reproduction.

Sexual union is often called "making love," and that is a good description. It says a lot about what's supposed to happen when a man and a woman share themselves sexually. One purpose of complete sexual union is to "make" even more love than was there before, to celebrate and deepen it.

With a little thought, you can see another purpose. Making love can also make a baby. Babies and children need lots of nonstop love for a long time in order to become complete, mature human beings who are now also able to love genuinely.

Total sexual sharing . . . deepening an already committed love . . . helping create new life and caring for that new life — all together, they fit perfectly into a permanent relationship called marriage. That's how God planned it.

Not everybody in the world you live in sees it that way. You have to decide whose view of sex you will adopt.

See, human sexual equipment will function whether there's a permanent loving relationship or not. It's like any other power you have. God didn't make it impossible to move your arms if you're trying to hurt somebody. Your tongues don't get tied in knots whenever you're about to cuss somebody out. Your sexual parts are no different. That's why it's such a joke when people have sex to prove their manhood or womanhood. They haven't proven anything except that their bodies work — they can have sex. Big deal. So can everybody.

There are many names for casual sex, ranging from very crude words on through the frequent term, "doing it." Think about the difference between the phrases "making love" and "doing it." They tell you a lot.

Dogs and cats, mice and moose, chipmunks and gorillas "do it." Any *animal* can *do it*.

Human beings who are committed to each other forever *make love*. There's a huge difference.

22. Feeling OK About You and Your Body? (Yes, Including....)

"Hello again, Mr. Snidley. This is your third visit this week."

"And just in time, too, Doctor. I rushed right over as soon as I saw the symptoms. I've got hyperpathologitis!"

"Hyperpath — Mr. Snidley, I've never even heard of that disease."

"That doesn't mean I don't have it, Doctor. I just know I have it. And there's other stuff, too. Isn't there a nasty inflammation on my earlobes?"

"Your earlobes look perfectly normal, Mr. Snidley."

"Then the inflammation must have traveled inward. That makes it more serious, doesn't it? And that old trouble with my pancreas is flaring up. I can feel it going thump-thump-th-*bump*. That's bad, isn't it?"

"You can feel your pancreas going —"

"Yeah, sure can. Kept me awake last night. Tell it to me straight, Doc. How long do I have?"

You've probably heard the word that describes poor Snidley, even if you can't spell it. "Hypochondriac." A person who is constantly and excessively worried about his or her health. At your age you are not likely to be a hypochondriac.

But it is possible when you're growing up to be more worried than you need to be about the following questions. You may never ask them out loud, but you may feel them deeply. *"Am I okay?"* And sometimes that becomes more specifically, *"Is my body (going to turn out) okay?"* And sometimes even, *"Are the you-know-what parts of my body normal?"*

Those aren't dumb questions. But kids worry about them more than they need to. And to get answers, many kids do something that's no real help. They compare themselves with others and use standards that don't really mean a whole lot.

Some girls get depressed because they and Dolly Parton don't have much in common. They keep hoping that someday they'll need a pair of parachutes for a bra. Some guys glance around the shower room, take

59

mental measurements, decide they're not normal, and wonder if there's a secret vitamin that will add lots of hair and growth.

All the wrong comparisons. Those kinds of comparisons have *nothing* to do with being normal and OK. Nothing. Nothing at all. Absolutely nothing. (Are you picking up a message here? *Nothing* — got it?)

"I'm OK because God made me OK." Now if you have any trouble believing that, will you please repeat it a few million times until believing it comes a little more easily? And don't just believe it in order to ease the pain from defects that you think you still have. That's sort of like taking a bunch of aspirin to cure a broken leg; medicine won't unbreak your leg. Believe it because it's true.

See, there's no one single way of being OK. There are millions of ways. And one of them is yours. All yours. Yours alone. You don't have to be like anybody else to be OK, and, in particular, your body doesn't have to be like anybody else's.

For an interesting study, make a list of well-known people who were considered physically perfect — people who had other people practically drooling over their bodies. And then make a list of the divorces, suicides, addictions, nervous breakdowns, and general emotional garbage that went along with having those "perfect" bodies. You may be very glad you're not a 10 + . If you don't have the kind of body they put on the covers of sex magazines, if your phone isn't ringing every night with calls from people who would like to spend time — preferably very alone — with you, you're fine. You're not a sexual failure or any other kind of failure.

It's important to believe this about yourself, to have faith in the person God created: you. Someone who doesn't believe it may try to "prove" his or her okayness simply by having sex. It's a simple "proof," except that it just doesn't prove anything. Anybody can have sex.

People who don't believe they're OK may also feel they have to reward anybody who seems interested in them, to put out a little in order to keep that other person interested. This is like walking around with a huge pin that says, "I don't think very much of me."

Keep coming back to the basic idea: God made you OK, including your sexuality. You and God can work out your life together. You do *not* need the approval or advice of peers who try to judge and run your life, including your sexuality.

You may read a newspaper or magazine summary of somebody's "study of today's sexuality." Some such studies are honest and intended to help; others are just glorified garbage. In either case, the reports often mention teenagers who are "sexually active" — meaning they "do it."

It can sound as though *those* kids are the normal ones. As though they're the ones who have dared to be different, who have reached out to experience real life, who have hit the big leagues and proved they're worth something. And the same kind of doubts can hit you when one of your peers says, "You haven't scored yet? Haven't even gotten to second base? Wow, that's a little . . . strange. You sure you're not gay or something?"

Learn to recognize pure nonsense when you hear it. You just heard an example right there.

You're not sexually active? And you don't intend to be until it's right?

Congratulations on being normal. Don't ever worry about whether or not you're OK. You're following the plan God intended. *That's* called being normal and OK.

SECTION EIGHT:
ON THE
HOME FRONT

23. Home Is Where We Learn About Going Home

I found my Dad dead in a chair in his apartment one Monday afternoon. The television was still on. Since he rarely watched TV in the daytime, he must have died the night before, apparently peacefully.

Ironically, I was in the middle of a writing assignment on "The Home." It hadn't been going well. The things I put on paper were like pistons operating out of sync in an engine — jerky and rough.

But losing my Dad brought lots of feelings about "home." One was that Dad had gone "home" to heaven. Another was how home here on earth is a preparation for home in heaven.

God fills life with neat things and they're all messages, like previews of an upcoming movie called *Eternity*. Every genuinely good thing here on earth — roller coasters, pizzas, Christmas trees, hugs, and swimming pools — is God's way of saying, "Enjoy — but you haven't seen anything yet. Wait until you catch my next act. It's called heaven."

Home is another one of those neat things that's a preview of heaven. But like everything else on earth, it's not perfect. Roller coaster rides end too quickly, Christmas trees begin to droop, some days at the pool cause sunburn, and some pizzas cause heartburn.

But since home is where you spend a lot of time until you begin adult life on your own, you may want it to be more perfect than it is or even can be. That can make you blind to the many good things about your home, while you see very vividly all the things that aren't perfect.

If your mother loses patience, you may forget the countless meals she fixed when she didn't feel like it, and all the times she searched for missing shoes and boots and jackets and ball gloves. When your father seems to ignore something you did right, you forget the times he fixed your bicycle and drove you to dozens of ball games, swimming parties, and movies. It's not easy to appreciate what you have in your home just because they're not perfect.

Sure, things can go awfully wrong in a home. It may break up with a bitter divorce. Even a "friendly" divorce isn't easy to take. A parent may become alcoholic or abusive. It's dumb to say things like that don't hurt. They do and the hurt is often deep even though you may pretend otherwise. (The most common remark I hear from kids who are really hurting from something at home is, "But it doesn't really bother me.")

But with lots of vision, you can see even the bad parts as another kind of message from God — a message saying, "Try to learn from what's happening; do your best to keep it from repeating in the home *you* make." And even then it isn't either right or healthy to spend all your time tossing accusations at those people who couldn't quite make home work perfectly, even though they may have tried pretty hard.

And home, remember, isn't simply something that happens to you. It's something you help make. Any place called "home" is the result of what everybody living there puts into it. Everybody. A good question to ask is, "Am I simply expecting home to be terrific, or am I helping to *make* it as good as it can be?"

24. Zap and You're Changed

That's one of the most common themes in stories — from classic literature down through comic books and TV. Zap and you're changed. Cinderella pads around in rags, gets zapped, and turns into the chick of the century dressed in designer stuff. Clark Kent becomes Superman, Dr. Jekyll becomes Mr. Hyde, Dr. David Banner becomes the Incredible Hulk, frogs become handsome princes. Sometimes the change is from good to bad, sometimes from bad to good, sometimes just from one thing to another. There's something about this instant change theme that is entertaining, even though it doesn't happen in real life.

Well, not usually. There's the case of "zap-and-you're-changed" that is somewhat believable. It goes like this.

Once upon a time a guy and a girl meet, like each other, start going together, fall in love, and marry. For a while, they're real, regular people. They know what's happening; they know how to enjoy life; they have a good idea of what things are all about.

Then one day they turn into parents.

They look the same, but suddenly they stop living in the real world. They start worrying about dumb things like cutting the grass and keeping the house in order. The fun of staying up late and turning the music up loud gets erased from their memory banks.

OK, so that's an exaggeration. But it might come fairly close to the way you see your parents at times. Sometimes you wish you could zap them back into "real" people.

But there's a problem with what's "real." People tend to think "real" means "just like me."

Take food, for example. After a month in the Orient, you might say, "I can't wait to get back to some *real* food," and you'd probably mean hamburgers and pizza. But a Chinese person, after a month of hamburgers and pizza, would also say, "I can't wait to get back to some *real* food."

Many things make a person different from others, and growing up is one of them. Already you're not the same as you were only a short time ago. You've probably passed the stage of playing with dolls or sneaking a pet frog into the house. But don't forget there was a time when such things were *real* and important to you.

In the years to come, each stage will seem like "This is what it's all about" while you're there. Even when you stay the same, the world around you will change. Believe it or not, a scene like the following will happen: You'll be playing the albums or tapes you grew up with, the music you love right now, *the* really great music . . . and your kids will come up and say, "Aw, Mom/Dad, how can you stand that *old-fashioned stuff*?"

So it shouldn't be surprising that your parents are different from you. It's not bad either. For proof, try to imagine your parents acting exactly like you and your friends — same interests, same activities, same way of talking and acting.

Would you really want to come home and find your Mom practicing cheerleading in the middle of the kitchen, waving pompoms and chewing bubble gum? Would your Dad seem like a real Dad if he stood in front of the bathroom mirror flexing his muscles from a dozen different angles to see if he was enough of a hunk?

Most teenagers wouldn't really want their parents to be just like them. But that means teens have to accept their parents as different, accept them for what and who they are — real people. Real people who are trying to do a pretty tough job.

Think of something you've been in charge of. Anything, it doesn't matter. You wanted it to be right, even though it wouldn't last forever. Think of the feelings you had at each stage: starting out hoping for the best . . . growing a little worried when things didn't work out . . . getting tired of the hassle now and then . . . then picking up the pieces and making a fresh start.

Now try those same feelings and imagine that you're in charge of a *human being* . . . a person who *will* last forever. And imagine that you care a lot about what happens to that human being — enough to say "Absolutely not" when it would be a lot easier to be a cool hero and say "Okay, go ahead."

"Ain't easy bein' in charge of a young 'un — but I wouldn't trade it," a parent from a small town in northern Georgia remarked to me once. He was right.

There's a really decent chance your parents know what they're talking about. God gave us only ten commandments. "Honor your father and mother" is one of them. Something that makes God's top ten must be pretty important.

SECTION NINE:
YOU DON'T LIVE IN A VACUUM

25. Getting Off the Hook/ Putting Somebody Else On

"He started it."

"It was her idea."

"They dared me."

"He told me to do it."

"Some friends of mine did the same thing last week, but they got away with it. It's not fair."

Sound familiar? You've heard all these excuses and many more. Human beings love to get off the hook; they've been doing it ever since Adam tried to justify himself in that nasty incident with the forbidden fruit. In fact, Adam even sought to place part of the blame on God himself: "The woman whom *you put here* with me — *she* gave me fruit from the tree, and so I ate it" (Genesis 3:12).

This same ploy has been used in situations ranging from kid stuff to international horror. Third-graders use it to excuse a tossed paper wad. Nazi officials described their mass murdering of Jews as simply "following orders."

Now nobody really has so much power over you that once he or she does something wrong, you have to follow and imitate and be a part of it. Saying "*He* did it first, so I *had* to do it, too" is the same as announcing, "I acted like a robot."

But there is a serious aspect to this business of "*He* started it" and "*She* said it was okay." How you act does have a great influence on how others act, probably far more than you ever realized.

Human beings are great imitators. They get ideas from watching and listening to one another. This certainly isn't always bad. It's part of being human. God intended for you to learn from others, and it's great when you learn something worthwhile. But when an action tempts someone else to sin, that's a different ball game entirely, and it has a name: "scandal."

Sometimes scandal is very obvious and up front: a direct invitation to do something wrong.

"We're gonna see how much each of us can rip off from Woolworth's. You gotta come, man — unless you want everybody to know you're chicken." That's scandal of a very heavy, very evil sort. It often happens when people know that what they're planning is really wrong, but if they can get some others to join them, it seems to spread the responsibility around and each one doesn't feel quite so guilty. (That's garbage, though: Each one is just as guilty as if he or she had done the whole thing alone.)

At other times, scandal can be indirect, not even intended. If your little brother sees you preparing a cheat sheet for tomorrow's test or smells booze on your breath, that's scandal, too. And once the damage is done, it's extremely hard to repair. You can't fix it simply by saying, "Hey, don't *you* do this." In fact, no amount of opposite-message words can overcome the effect of a bad example. The saying is really true that "Your actions scream so loud I can't hear your words."

Scandal is a powerful force. People often look not just for excuses to explain something they did, but for reasons or encouragement to do something they're tempted to do. And "reasons" often given for things like getting buzzed, getting into sex, stealing, and cheating are often some form of "*They* do it, so why can't I? It can't be that bad."

Jesus had something to say about scandal in Matthew 18:6-7. Look it up, but be ready for a shock. This is one of those times Jesus was about as gentle as a sledgehammer.

There's a good side to example. People notice and copy good actions, too. They probably won't come up and tell you that they were inspired to do something neat because they saw you doing something similar. But you can be pretty certain that your good influence is rubbing off somewhere, even if you don't know where and can't see it.

Imagine you have a fan club, younger kids who look up to you and know a lot about you. Picture one of them saying the following: "For a whole year, I've tried to be exactly like _____ (your name here), and now I've become. . . . "

What good or bad qualities would end their sentences?

26. What's the Difference? Ask Rick and Lisa and Brad

Early in life, Stan picked up a "What difference does it make?" way of looking at many things. When he was nine, a friend dared him to steal five bucks from his mother's purse. Stan knew it was wrong, but his friend kept saying, "What difference does it make — your folks have lots of money anyway." So he took the five bucks. His mother didn't miss it. Although he knew better, Stan began to think maybe it *didn't* make any difference.

In junior high, a bunch of Stan's friends were cheating like crazy on tests whenever they could get away with it. "What difference does it make?" they said. "Nobody needs to know this boring stuff anyway." It wasn't long before that began to make sense to Stan.

When he was thirteen, Stan really beat up a kid. He was starting to feel bad about it, but some other guys said, "He was a jerk, so what difference does it make if you beat him up?" It was easier to believe that than to feel guilty. So Stan agreed, "Yeah, what difference does it make?"

By the time he was sixteen, "What's the difference?" was Stan's usual way of looking at practically everything. He cut a lot of classes and ignored a lot of assignments because it "didn't make any difference." He barely made it through school, but he did just make it, even though he hadn't learned much. That didn't bother him, though, because what difference did learning things make?

Those are a few things. There were lots of others and, as you can guess, they all "didn't make any difference." The only thing that made a difference was whether or not Stan was having a good time.

Stan's twenty-four now, and he has no regrets about anything he's done or hasn't done. Can you guess why? Right.

But it did make a big difference to Rick. Rick got his start on heavy drinking from Stan. Stan drinks too much himself, although he claims he's not an alcoholic — not yet anyway. But Rick is. He's twenty-three, burned-out, and he pretty much lives for the next drink.

Rick's wife and baby girl take a distant second place to good old J.D. It started with Stan telling him how cool it was to get really buzzed.

It made a difference to Lisa. Stan pressured her into sex back in senior year. He told her that everybody was doing it, and if she didn't go along she wasn't normal. After a few times, they had a huge argument about it. She wanted to stop; Stan didn't. So Stan dropped her. But he also spread stories about things they did plus a few other things he added. Very quickly, Lisa got a rotten reputation. Many guys wouldn't ask her out and those who did only wanted one thing. To put it mildly, it messed up her life.

There's also Miss Thompson. She was Stan's history teacher in the tenth grade, first semester. It was her first year of teaching and she wasn't exactly an old pro at handling a classroom. Stan thought it was a real trip to take advantage of this. He organized a campaign to drive her crazy every day. It worked, too. She quit in midyear. Stan used to brag that he and his class gave the new teacher a nervous breakdown. With a little experience, Miss Thompson would have been a great teacher because she knew her subject, she was creative, and she really cared about kids. Lots of young people would have benefited from being in her classroom. But it'll never happen now.

And then there's Brad. That's Stan's kid. He's three and a half, a neat little kid. Brad deserves to have a decent father, a man, a *real* man, who sets an example of how to be a strong, loving, caring human being, a Christian. But he won't get it.

Oh, Stan enjoys showing his kid off now and then to his drinking buddies. But that's about as far as his fatherhood goes. He figures he brings home the paycheck, so he's doing his job. What difference does anything else make?

The way things are going, there'll be a divorce before long. Brad deserves better than that. So does Mary, Stan's wife.

How a person acts: Does it matter to anybody aside from that person himself or herself? Does it . . . make any difference?

You know what Stan would say.

What do *you* say?

27. Will the Real You Please Stand Out?

See if you can identify what these people have in common.

First, there's Horatio. Horatio comes to school and swaggers around with a sneer on his face, saying, "I'm *bad*, man. I'm *real* bad. Back off, everybody." He wears his shirt open and has a bunch of fake hair glued to his chest.

Second, there's Sirenella. She never walks anywhere — she sways and swivels. She wears three ounces of mascara, two shades of lip gloss, fluorescent orange nail polish, five earrings per ear, and designer label leg warmers.

Next, there's Ellington. He likes to mention things which you're supposed to find fascinating — like his SAT scores, which he claims put him in the top one percent of the population. He'll also let you know that his family has a huge pool in the backyard, a BMW in the driveway, and a personal letter from the mayor.

Finally, there's Nearcoma. She walks around with slumped shoulders and often a limp. She coughs every ninety seconds, talks in a faint whisper, and bends over in apparent pain at her desk. Doctors have said there's nothing wrong with her, but she still acts like a paramedic team ought to be following her around all day.

The question again is, "What do these people have in common?" *Besides* being strange.

They aren't happy with themselves, that's what. They don't think their real self is good enough.

Horatio doesn't think he's masculine enough, so he puts on an act to convince both himself and everybody else that he's bad news for anyone who gets in his way. Sirenella doesn't think she's feminine enough, so she's trying to give her sex appeal a little help. Ellington feels the need to boost his ego by claiming to come from a higher, better class of people than those he associates with at high school. And Nearcoma doesn't feel she gets enough attention just being herself; being "sick" is one way of getting the extra attention she wants.

"But nobody acts *that* weird," you may be thinking. You're right. The above characters are exaggerations. They're exaggerated to illustrate the masks, the acts, that people hide behind. But those masks, those acts, *are* real. True, you don't know any guys who put fake hair on their chests and walk around chanting, "I'm bad." But you have met lots of guys (and some girls) who try to "be somebody" by acting tough, threatening other people, and pushing them around. That's the same thing.

What's all this have to do with growing up Christian? A lot. People who don't feel OK about themselves nearly always take it out on others in some way or other — name-calling, put downs, gossip, violence. Masks and games like those above aren't just harmless Halloween stunts.

Another reason is that these masks and games can keep you distant from God. You instinctively know that he sees through them. Your phony ways won't work with God and you realize that. But since it's hard to drop them, you might find it easier to avoid God completely rather than risk being completely real. Your masks make it hard for God to get through to you, too. It's as difficult to feel God's love when you're walking around being phony as it is to feel a hug when you're wearing a suit of iron.

"I'm OK because God made me, and God doesn't make junk."

That's not just a cute slogan. That's true. If you really believed it, you wouldn't play so many games and wear so many masks . . . and you'd be a lot happier.

SECTION TEN:
HONESTLY!
(THAT'S A
GOOD IDEA!)

28. Who Is the Thief?

"Girl Returns Lost Billfold, $700"
"Man Finds Diamond Bracelet Worth Millions — Hands It Over"
Every now and then you see headlines like these. What's your reaction? You don't have to make a public speech about it, but you should know where you stand on something like this.

Here's one possible reaction:

"That's really stupid. Those people should have kept the stuff. Who'd ever find out? If people are dumb enough to lose a billfold or a bracelet, that's *their* problem."

Here's an opposite one:

"Those people did the right thing, the *only* thing to do in a situation like that. If something doesn't belong to you, you don't take it. And if you find it, you give it back. It's that simple."

And here are some in-between, trying-to-have-it-both-ways reactions:

"I'd keep the money or maybe half of it — after all, I'd deserve a reward — and send the billfold back in the mail so the person wouldn't have to get a new driver's license and other stuff."

"A woman who has a diamond bracelet like that can afford to lose it. She'll just buy another one. So I'd sell the bracelet, but then give some of the money to a worthy cause."

OK, decision time. Which of these reactions is yours?

"It depends. Like, if your family was starving or if your kid needed expensive medicine you couldn't buy. . . . "

OK, things like that change the situation. But why talk about one case (out of a thousand) that isn't likely to happen at all? What would you do with the billfold or the bracelet? In regular, old, ordinary, everyday life, does it really "depend?" Well, in a way it does.

It depends on whether or not you're a thief.

Taking or keeping things that don't belong to you is incredibly easy to "rationalize." That means inventing phony reasons to make yourself feel better about doing something you know very well is wrong. Here are

75

three common ways people rationalize stealing, whether it's actually going out and taking something, or keeping an item they happen to find or receive but which they know belongs to someone else.

1. *"It actually belongs to me anyway."*

Example: You know, when you think about it, this store rips customers off all the time. Look at the prices around here — they're terrible! They probably make a thousand percent profit on all this stuff. With all the things I've bought here, I bet I've paid a couple hundred dollars more than I should have. Actually, if things were fair, *they owe me*. So if I sort of take this camera along with me when I leave, it's not actually stealing. I'm just taking part of what they owe me.

2. *"Nobody's going to get hurt."*

Example: People in this part of town have money. I mean *real* money. They're loaded. So what's it matter if I rip off this ten-speed? The kid that owns it won't be hurting — his old man will just buy him another one. So if nobody gets hurt, it's not wrong. In fact, the kid will probably get a better one than he has now — so actually I'm doing him a favor.

Another example: Look, the people won't have to pay for this. Their insurance will. That's what they got insurance for. And insurance companies are rich — everybody knows that. So nobody's getting hurt and that means it's not wrong.

3. *"I need or deserve it more than they do."*

Example: What does Warbucks do to earn all that money he always walks around with? Not a blasted thing. His parents just give it to him. Me, I work my rear end off around the house all the time and I still have to beg for every buck I need. If things were fair, I'd have gotten paid this $10 here in Warbuck's locker. So if I take it, I'm just making things fair, the way they should be to start with.

What do all these have in common?

They're all excuses that thieves use to keep themselves from *feeling* like thieves.

29. Nobody Needs to Be a Fraud

According to an often-told story, the circus owner, P. T. Barnum, once had a problem in the tent that housed his wild animal display. Many people had never seen wild animals before so they stood there fascinated and wouldn't leave. Soon the tent became congested and people who were standing outside waiting to pay and go in got tired and went away.

Anything that cut into profits was very upsetting to P. T. Barnum. But he couldn't force people out of the tent. He had to find a way to get them to leave.

He came up with an idea. He had noticed that people seemed to think the female of a species was wilder and fiercer than the male. So his wild animals were the lioness, the tigress, the leopardess, and so forth. He put up a sign above a small corridor in the tent: "This Way To The Egress."

An egress! In a display all its own! It must be the meanest, fiercest, wildest wild animal of all! That's what many people thought, anyway, and that's what P. T. Barnum wanted them to think. They followed the sign and found themselves . . . outside. An egress is an exit.

Now, nobody marched P. T. Barnum down to municipal court and charged him with fraud. And supposedly the judges would have divided opinions on whether or not his sign amounted to fraud.

Regardless, "fraud" probably sounds like a strictly adult crime, something the FBI investigates, something that guys wearing suits and ties commit. And in a legal sense, fraud probably is an adult thing. Generally speaking, kids don't try to sell Pennsylvania residents two acres of "all-natural Florida real estate" that turn out to be swampland inhabited by alligators and a few billion tons of algae. But adults who do get convicted of phony real estate deals, broken contracts, etc., may have gotten their start much earlier in life.

It may have begun back in Miss Smith's fifth grade math class. Or Mr. Jones' ninth grade biology class. The whole ugly scene of fraud can start pretty early and then spread like a cancer.

It can begin with cheating — on tests, on book reports, on projects, on term papers, on almost anything you have to do in school. And that's fraud because anything you do there is supposed to reflect what you know, what you've actually done and earned.

Can you beat the system and get away with it? Can you come out looking cool or at least OK even though you didn't do or learn much? Depends on the teacher. You know that and so do I. Some teachers spot cheating techniques a mile away (like the twist-my-head-to-look-like-I'm-getting-something-out-of-my-eye-while-my-other-eye-checks-out-the-paper-on-the-next-desk), and others don't.

"Get real," people tell each other. Good advice. This all depends on how real you want to be.

God gave each of us a certain unique amount of ability to work with and then said, "Go out and make me proud of you." What you have is not exactly the same stuff he gave to other people and vice versa. That was a pretty good idea. Life would be terrifically boring if everybody were alike and everybody's accomplishments were automatic and identical.

What you do with your God-given ability is up to you. You can either work with it and be proud of what you genuinely accomplish, or you can try to beat the systems — cheat.

There are always reasons why *it's OK just this time*. "The test is unfair." "This is stupid stuff — nobody will ever need to know this garbage." "I didn't have time to study and it wasn't my fault." "If I get a bad grade, Dad will be really upset and that's bad for his heart." Ten million reasons why it's OK just this once. But it isn't. Soon all the OK-just-this-once's become a permanent way of looking at life: Beat the system — anytime you can get something for nothing, do it. If all of society is full of people whose goal is to beat the system, it won't take a professional sociologist to predict what will happen.

You can either be the real person God planned or just find an easy way to be somebody who looks OK on the outside. "I'm me and I'm real" versus "I'm a piece of cardboard that's painted up to look real."

You know which one God had in mind.

30. Your Credibility Rating

It's the bottom of the ninth inning in the final playoff game in the newly formed Continental Baseball League. The Boston Brontosauri lead the Tallahassee Pterodactyls 3-2. Pterodactyls batting, two outs, runners at first and third. If you're a Pterodactyl fan, your big concern is *"Who's up?"* The scoreboard flashes his name and his batting average: Sklodynski — he's hitting .392. All *right!* Based on past performance, there's a great chance Sklodynski will come through. You have confidence in him.

Now let's change the batter. Sklodynski isn't up; he's only on deck. Thworp is up — and he's hitting .107. Your confidence just fell into the pits, didn't it?

Every time you speak, people have the same feeling of confidence or lack of it about you. Like a batting average, your past performance in telling the truth or not telling the truth is the basis for their expectations. You've either acquired a reputation for telling the truth or for lying when it's convenient.

Call it a credibility rating. And once you've lost it, you've lost something big. Trust is not nickel-and-dime stuff. Trust is a really big item, and once you've lost it, it's awfully hard to get back. Like a batting average, it's based on many past performances. If a player has a .107 average after a hundred and fifty times at bat, he can blast the ball out of the park the next five times straight and he's still raised his average only to .135, not exactly an award-winning figure which will inspire the confidence of everyone.

Imagine a world where you know that anything you hear or read is the actual truth, except for totally unintentional misunderstandings. You'd get rid of a lot of doubt and fear and tension and hurt, wouldn't you? That's how God wanted it. Like all of his laws, the law about telling the truth is there because it makes life work right.

And, like any other God-given ability, the power of speech is not yours to use in any way you find convenient at the time. You have the power to move your arms and hands, but that doesn't mean you're free to use those powers to rearrange somebody's face or relocate somebody's wallet.

Are there ever exceptions to your obligation to state all of the facts exactly as they are? Of course. If you ask a friend to come over and help you with your math when actually you have a terrific surprise birthday party planned for that person, that's not an evil deed.

And if a guy you're pretty certain is a professional hit man asks where your neighbor (the district attorney) is, and you're pretty certain he'll use the information to waste your neighbor, it's OK to say you don't know even if you do. What makes the difference in this case is that the person asking the questions has no right to the truth. He's forfeited that right because of his intention to use the facts for an evil purpose.

But those exceptions just don't happen often. Some people like to think they do, though. With a little imagination, they can always dream up a reason why the other person "doesn't have a right to know the truth." As with cheating, there's always a "reason" to make it seem OK, or at least not so bad, on this particular occasion.

Saint Paul was as up front as you can possibly get on this in Colossians 3:9. "Stop lying to one another." Period.

Besides, something really nice happens when you follow God's law about telling the truth. Your credibility rating soars. And it's really great to be known as a person who tells it straight, no matter what.

31. To Be or Not to Be? The Real Thing

One of the things that hasn't changed since I was a kid is advertising aimed at kids. It's beamed through the TV and printed on the back covers of comic books and kids' magazines. A lot of it tries to sell toys and gadgets that, well, let's say the actual item often works much differently than it's pictured in the advertisement.

When I was about ten, I sent for a spy periscope that, according to the ad, would let me see around corners and over walls without being detected. The ad almost made it seem as though this was what the CIA used.

Finally it came, my fantastic spy periscope — a flimsy, cardboard tube with a top section that tilted on a couple tin rivets and a cheap metal mirror. It was big, clumsy, and it didn't reflect anything very clearly. The only creature I ever spied on without being instantly noticed was the dog and the dog was asleep at the time.

On another occasion, I sent for the "Draw-Anything-Like-An-Artist" device. I won't even try to describe how it was supposed to work, but it didn't. My artistic masterpieces still looked as though they had been drawn by a left-footed camel holding a right-footer's pencil.

Several years ago, my daughter went wild over a dancing doll that was being advertised every ninety seconds on Saturday morning TV. In the commercial, the doll looked as though it had been through fifteen years of professional dance training. In real life, all it did was swing one leg a little, turn around on the other, and fall over. After its long hair got caught in the turning mechanism, the *only* thing it did was fall over.

When this happens, we protest that it isn't fair. Products should look like the pictures that sell them and perform the way they promise. If an ad says "easy to assemble," the product should be easy to assemble. Companies should advertise fairly, deliver what they promise, and stand behind their products.

All true, and very easy to say about companies and manufacturers and stores.

What about *people?* What about you and me? If you were a store, what would your reputation be? Would people say, "That's a nice place. They treat you fairly and always give you a straight answer. They come through with what they promise and if something goes wrong, they make up for it."

Would people say, "At that store, they act friendly and they make things sound awfully good, but you have to be careful. They tend to exaggerate and you can't always depend on what they promise."

Would people say, "All that place wants to do is make a sale. They'll lie like crazy to get you in the store so they can rip you off a few times. After that, they don't even care what you think. They know there'll always be somebody else dumb enough to fall for what they say."

We're talking about a thing called "integrity." Some stores have it and some don't. Some people have it and some don't.

When you have integrity, people say and think this about you: "I may not always agree with that person. Sometimes we don't get along, or we may have different interests. But I know that in any contact we have, I'll never be lied to, cheated, misled, or used."

That's a great reputation to have.

Jesus had integrity. Even the people who disliked what he said knew they could count on him for straight answers, kept promises, and fair treatment. They knew he said what he believed and followed through on those beliefs.

That's the way it is with winners. Developing your integrity is a winning way to imitate the Lord.

SECTION ELEVEN:

OTHER FOLKS —
THEY LIVE
HERE, TOO

32. Tribes: Not Just an Old Indian Custom

You're in line for tickets to the concert. A bunch of people ahead of you get third row, center, stage-level seats, so you figure you should get pretty good tickets, too. But when you get to the window, the seller says there are only a few seats left, way up on the third level, in a corner. You protest.

"That's what we've got — take it or leave it," he says. So you buy the tickets — and then you notice that some people who were *behind* you in line also get third row, stage-level seats.

Later you learn the explanation. The people running the ticket office have friends. Those friends get the good seats, no matter when they show up. Other people get what's left.

That stinks, right?

Easy enough to understand when you're on the outside of a group, being treated unfairly by the people who are in it. But when you're on the inside, it's easy to forget. Do you respect the rights of your close friends more than the rights of other people? Good question to think about now and then.

This isn't the same as liking everybody equally. That's not going to happen and it isn't necessary in order for us to be good Christians. The point is this: When someone shows up here on planet earth as a human being, he or she has a certain worth and rights just for that reason: being a person. Whether you personally think that person is attractive, likable, intelligent, sensible, cool, fun to be with, or anything else doesn't matter.

If you forget that or ignore it, you'll treat only your friends, or only those who belong to your school, or your age group, or your race, or your whatever, as real people. Your "tribe." You might never think of lying to those people or stealing from them or deliberately hurting them. But other people? That doesn't seem so wrong. They're outsiders. And sometimes you see outsiders as not really people at all.

There's a good chance you've read the book and/or seen the movie, *The Outsiders*. Ponyboy and Soda and Johnny and all the other greasers weren't regarded as real, worthwhile people by most of the "nice" folks. They were looked on simply as walking pieces of bad news because they didn't live in the right neighborhood.

Jesus himself said that if you're nice only to people who already like you, what's the big deal about that? That's a piece of cake.

Try making a list of your "other" people. The ones who don't dress like you, talk like you, or share any of your interests. The ones who aren't in your recess/after school/weekend group. The ones who would make your eyeballs roll if you had to sit next to them in class.

How do you treat *them* (which includes how you talk about them when they're not around)?

According to Jesus, *that's* where your Christianity shows.

33. World War III. Well, Close. Let's Not Have It

Kathy is having a party Saturday night. Maybe a dozen people. An ordinary party.

Usually Julie would be invited. Julie is one of Kathy's close friends. No, *used to be* one of Kathy's close friends. Julie isn't invited to this party. Deliberately.

Why? Something Julie said. Well, actually Kathy doesn't know for sure that Julie said it. She knows that Gail and Debbie *said* that Julie said it. But that's enough for Kathy. When she thinks people are out to get her, Kathy doesn't require much evidence. In fact, if there's no evidence at all that anybody is out to get her for any reason, she'll often make some up. Kathy loves a war. It seems she's not happy unless there's at least a minor battle going on.

Actually, she hadn't been planning a party at all until this happened. For one thing, she can't really afford it. To finance the party, she'll have to use some money she was saving to buy a new pair of expensive jeans. But the party seems like a good way to get back at Julie.

OK, so Kathy is already involved in staging something she doesn't really want to do. Let's leave her there and look at a couple very different ways that Julie can act in this situation. We'll call them Plan A and Plan B. Not very imaginative names, I know, but they're easy to keep straight.

Plan A
Julie hears from her friend, Mary, that she's deliberately not invited to Kathy's party. "Kathy's a jerk," Mary says.

"No, she's not really a jerk," Julie answers. "She's just mad and acting pretty stupid. She's trying to get back at me. There's really nothing for her to get back at, though. I didn't say what she thinks I said."

"What are you going to do about it?" Mary asks. Mary can't wait to hear what Julie plans in counter-revenge and maybe be a part of it.

"Why should I *do* anything about it?" Julie asks. "She'll get over it."

"Aren't you hurt?"

"Sure, but I'm not gonna have a spasm over it. So I miss a party. I couldn't have gone anyway. I have to babysit."

"I guess you're going to forgive her for acting like a jerk?" Mary asks, unbelieving.

"Yeah, I guess so. Why not?"

Mary looks puzzled; she can't figure Julie out. But Julie walks away feeling OK.

Plan B

Mary delivers the same message. "Kathy's a jerk," Mary says.

"Jerk is too nice a word for her!" Julie mutters. "And she's not getting away with it, either. She is going to be *so sorry* she ever opened her mouth!" Julie's face looks as though somebody put tabasco sauce on her Cheerios.

It's fourth bell, lunch. Julie has a big Spanish test coming up next bell and she was going to spend some time after lunch on last minute review because she needs a good grade on this test.

But she can't think about that now. There's something else much more important: She has to find out exactly who has been invited to Kathy's party. Then, when she finds out, she has to guess who might be more loyal to her than to Kathy. It's a tricky decision. She comes up with three names: Traci, Ann, and Kim. Now she has to track down each of them and try to talk them out of going to Kathy's party.

She succeeds with Traci. For a couple minutes she feels a little better. She chalks up a name on "her side."

But Ann says, "Well, I guess if you're invited to a party, you should go. I mean, I'm sorry you weren't invited, but I can't do anything about that." Julie immediately labels Ann "enemy," along with Kathy. Now she has two people to get back at.

She can't find Kim. She spends a lot of time wondering what Kim would have said. There's so much acid in her gut (and in her heart and on her tongue) she ought to audition for a Hyper-Strength Digel commercial.

Consequently, she blows the Spanish test. She doesn't even have time to finish it because she spends two minutes here and three minutes there rehearsing exactly what she'll do and say the next time she meets Kathy. She mentally practices the look on her face and the tone of her voice.

During last bell she writes a note to give to Jan to give to Kim at the bus stop. It's full of nasty stuff about Kathy, most of it made up. But a teacher sees the note being passed. Julie's busted and has to spend time in detention.

This drives her crazy. It's not just the idea of detention; she can handle that. But today it's a waste of valuable time which she had planned to spend calling a half dozen people . . . trying to figure out who's on her side and who isn't, who's going to the party and who isn't, who's heard what from whom and who hasn't . . . etc.

Her whole life has become a war map, full of allies and enemies, battle positions and weapons, fear and doubt, tension and hate. She's trying so hard to win her little war that she's ending up a colossal loser.

Compare this with Plan A, where she simply forgave Kathy and went on with her life.

Forgiveness: Jesus knew what he was talking about when he recommended it.

34. Some Off-the-Wall Ideas

Psst! Want to know where UFO's really come from? Not from outer space at all. No! They come from *inner* space. That's right. A race of superior beings lives inside the hollow core of the earth. Now and then, they come outside to check out what's happening on the surface. Their secret openings to the interior of the earth are located beneath the polar ice caps.

No, that isn't really my idea. But I didn't make it up either. A guy wrote a whole hardback book trying to prove that theory of UFO's. As far as I know, the United Nations did not send an international team to search out the secret polar trapdoors and cement them shut. Not too many people, in general, took that off-the-wall idea very seriously, either.

But sometimes a wild, far-out, off-the-wall, just plain wrong idea does gain wide acceptance and huge crowds of people brainlessly swallow it. Here's an example: To be really tough, cool, independent, important, and worth something, you make other people hurt. You make fun of them, put them down, make them afraid of you, or just generally ignore them like an ant or a worm or anything else you consider dumb and worthless. You prove how capable and worthwhile you are by walking through life like a flamethrower — calling the shots, getting your way, and leaving hurt feelings in your path. If the other people are bigger or have more authority, you say stuff about them behind their backs, or you do little things to irritate them, stopping just short of getting busted.

Where did this idea come from? Is it a hangover from caveman days? Does it come from movies where the coolest heroes are people who leave the most blood in their path? Or perhaps from TV situation comedies where one out of every three or four laughs comes from somebody insulting somebody else?

How did loving and caring get stuck with an image of weakness? Loving shows *weakness?!?* Even the idea of alien beings driving their UFOs in and out of the North Pole makes more sense than *that*.

But people often choose the easier of two ways to go. That explains why there are more put downs than compliments. That explains why there's more revenge than forgiveness going around. That explains why more people walk by than stop when a person needs help.

Put downs and name calling and bullying and gossiping and getting revenge and deliberately ignoring — they're all a piece of cake. A total piece of cake. Nothing to it. Hurting people is easy. It takes no courage, no talent, no class.

Loving and caring about people calls for being tough. It means being genuinely cool. It takes class. It's easier to be selfish and destructive than to be caring and loving — just as it's easier to walk down a hill into a garbage dump than to climb a mountain.

The world can use more tough-minded mountain climbers. How about being one?

35. Someone...Or Something

Most people welcome a chance to find out what others really think of them. People often are not up front with their feelings about each other, so we often remain in the dark about the impressions we make on others. Most people are afraid to say, "The way you act really turns me off" or too shy to say, "I think you're really special and wonderful."

So when the chance comes to overhear other people talking about us, we usually listen with the same careful attention we had when somebody first talked to us about sex. We hang on to every word.

Picture these two imaginary situations. First, let's say your name is Bill Thompson. You come back to the school building a few minutes after dismissal to get a notebook you forgot. You realize there's a group of teachers in the room — discussing *you*.

"Thompson's a pretty good choice for the citizenship award, don't you think?"

"Decent choice, I guess. But I don't know if we should pick him."

"Why not?"

"Well, there's publicity and pictures. Thompson's not the greatest looking kid, you know. I mean, he's not ugly, but he doesn't have a fresh, clean-cut look. The school's image is a factor here, too, you know."

"Good point. Is Thompson athletic?"

"Another minus. He played a little reserve basketball, but that's about it. Makes a better impression on the public if you can get a kid who's a good citizen and a good jock at the same time."

"True. What's his father do?"

"Dunno. Family's separated, I think."

"Well, that ices it. We gotta have a kid from a stable family. Makes a good photo when you got a smiling parent on each side of the kid."

Now let's say your name is Lisa and you're going with a guy named Matt. You also stop outside the classroom door because inside the room Matt and his friend Jay are talking — about you.

"You still going with Lisa?" Jay asks.

"Yeah, for a while yet. But it's about time for a change. I mean, Lisa's all right, but she's not a 10, you know."

"Really. Great legs, though."

"Yeah — fantastic legs. But the rest is sort of ordinary."

"Who you going after?"

"Shelly. Now *there's* a 10, man!"

"More like a 20. You gonna get her?"

"No problem. It'll take maybe a couple more weeks, but no problem. Some chicks you gotta work on gradually."

"When you gonna drop Lisa?"

"Soon as Shelly says she'll go with me. But till then I gotta have somebody for the weekend, you know."

If you're Bill or Lisa, how do you feel? There's hardly a word for it, is there? "Angry" doesn't even come close. Even "furious" seems weak. And hurt. Very, very hurt.

The teachers are talking about Bill Thompson — and kids in general — as though they were things, not persons. Bill's worth as a person and his worthiness for the award don't really matter. The teachers are looking for an exhibition, a showpiece to help give their school a good reputation. Their conversation centers around what kind of exhibit will impress the public.

Jay and Matt are talking about Lisa — and girls in general — in the same way: *objects* to be used. To Matt, Lisa isn't a girl; she's a body. She isn't a friend; she's a piece of property. He's about to throw her out in the same way he'd scrap an old concert jersey when a newer, wilder group makes it to the top.

That's what causes the hurt and the anger, and it's also what makes these situations so wrong. Lisa and Bill are being used . . . treated like objects.

People have a special value and they have rights. To infringe on their rights makes many ordinary actions wrong. If you pick a beautiful flower growing along the edge of the highway, that's fine. But if you go into somebody's yard and take a flower, that's a different matter even though it's the same physical action. In this case, it's called stealing because there's a person involved. A person owned the flower and had a right to keep it.

Trouble is, it's so easy to forget the rights and values of other persons. It's easy to treat them as objects. There are so many people in the world that people begin to seem ordinary.

If you found a diamond out of a million pebbles in your back yard, you'd treasure it — or sell it for a lot of money. Why? There aren't many diamonds. But if your back yard (and everybody else's) was littered with diamonds lying all over the place, they'd seem ordinary. They'd *be* ordinary, not particularly valuable at all.

But it doesn't work that way with people. Having millions of them running around planet Earth doesn't make any single one of them less valuable. Each is created in the image of God. Jesus said the way you treat other people (especially those you find it hard to get along with) is the indication of how much you love him.

How can you tell if you're respecting others as persons instead of using them as objects? Jesus gave you an excellent guideline. In fact, it's foolproof.

You're a person, right? And you know very well how *you'd* like to be respected and treated. So Jesus put it very simply in Matthew 7:12: "Treat others the way you would have them treat you."

36. Christian ... And Tough, Too?

"You're a jerk!"

"You're a *double* jerk!"

"I ain't scared of you!"

"You better be scared of me. I can beat you up bad!"

"I can beat you up badder!"

"Oh yeah?"

"Yeah!"

Who are these speakers? Two kids about, oh, seven years old. The scene is a school playground. Listen in on a little more of the dialogue and, for heaven's sake, don't laugh. This is serious stuff.

"You couldn't beat up an ant."

"Yeah I could! I could beat up an ape! You couldn't beat up a lightning bug!"

"I could beat up a tiger! And I can beat you up really super bad!"

(Hush — I told you not to laugh!)

It's time for the confrontation. Kid A makes a couple of fists and moves toward Kid B. Kid B backs off a half step and starts to circle around. This gives Kid A some confidence, so he moves in with his fists revolving like an off-center windmill. Kid B protects his head with his forearms and decides to attack from below. He kicks. He looks a little bit like he's practicing the Charleston or trying out for a chorus line.

What caused this battle of the Titans? Serious stuff once again. Kid A accused Kid B of having big ears. So Kid B accused Kid A of being stupid in spelling.

Your reactions, please.

You'd probably laugh at those two little kids standing there trying to act like tough, professional fighting machines capable of wiping out enemies. If only they knew how dumb they looked, right?

Let's say one kid grabs the other's lunch box and starts jumping up and down on it. You'd probably say that's wrong. Parents paid good money for it and destroying it is wrong. Plus the kid is just plain acting like a little jerk. And obviously nothing is being proven about excessive ear size or spelling skills.

Dumb. Pointless. Silly. Wrong.

Easy to see when you're watching seven-year-olds.

So why does the same thing seem OK, reasonable, worthwhile — even dramatic and admirable — when people get older?

Let's add seven to ten years or so to our pair of kids. This will change the situation considerably. How? Well, now the kids are likely to be fighting over a girl friend instead of an insult about big ears. Or because each one wants a "toughest guy on the turf" reputation. And now they're capable of actually doing some serious physical damage to each other. Now it's likely to be a ten-speed bike that's getting smashed instead of a lunch box.

That's how it is now that they're older.

That makes it OK?

It's just as dumb, just as pointless, just as silly, just as wrong — in fact, much more so because a couple of fifteen or seventeen-year-olds should think and act a little straighter than seven-year-olds. Violence is totally opposed to everything Jesus taught.

Now this may seem like a paid commercial message on behalf of Christian wimpitude. It's not. There is a distinction between force and violence.

If you break up a fight (whether you're being attacked or whether someone else is) by pinning the attacker to the ground and putting his arms in a hammerlock until he decides fighting wasn't such a cool idea after all, that's one thing. Call it force. Just enough force to stop the aggressive action, no more. Fine.

But if you go further and bloody his face (and later wreck his ten-speed), that's violence and it's wrong, absolutely dead wrong.

Being a Christian does not mean being a wimp. But you can't be a Christian and be into plain violence at the same time.

SECTION TWELVE:
SAINT _____
(PLEASE PRINT
CLEARLY)
YES, *YOU!*

37. You Didn't Really Say "Holiness," Did You?

Taking a trip back through time is always fun, even though you do it only through a book or a movie. In this trip, you'll see some kids from years ago. Here's one coming up on the screen right now. See him there in the classroom? His teacher is freaking out because the kid isn't adding common math problems very well. He doesn't seem too interested in learning how to do it, either. This kid is definitely not the mathematical type, right? If our mathematical-scientific future depends on him, we'd better head back for the caveman days, right? Who *is* that not-too-swift kid, by the way?

That was Albert Einstein. The twentieth-century mathematical and scientific genius.

Good thing *he* didn't believe in the way he looked to other folks back when he was a school kid.

Here's another one, a little older — senior year of high school. He wants to make a career of football. A scout from one of the biggest name colleges in the country is looking at him right now and making notes on his scouting report. Let's peek at the notes. They say, "Too small, too skinny to play football." Wow, that's a shame. Too bad the kid isn't the football type. Who *is* that kid, by the way?

Johnny Unitas. According to sportswriters, one of the five best quarterbacks of all time.

Here's a girl who likes science and wants to become a scientist. But back in her days, girls didn't become scientists. Look at all those people telling her that! A girl scientist — what a dumb idea, they're trying to tell her. Let's hope she doesn't believe them.

She didn't. That was Madame Curie. After over five hundred painstaking experiments, she isolated the element radium — a world-shaking scientific breakthrough.

And here's a baby-faced little boy. He's a server at church and right now he's carrying a candle in a solemn procession. What a nice — wait a minute, did you see *that?* He jabbed that candlestick into the ribs of the other server next to him! What awful behavior! Kids like that shouldn't be allowed to serve in church. Obviously he's not even close to the religious type. Who is that kid anyway?

Well, later in life he became known as Pope Pius XII.

What's true of all these people? They didn't lock themselves or let themselves be locked into little boxes called "I'm not the type."

Sometimes people do that to themselves. You, for example, may get a couple of bad grades in math or English and then decide, "I'm no good at this. I'm just not the type." You make a couple of mistakes in practice or in a game and decide, "I'm no good at this sport. I'm just not the type."

But that's like taking an emotional aspirin. If you don't do well at something, saying "I'm just not the type" makes you feel a little better. After all, if you're not "the type" for something, who can blame you when you don't do it well?

Sometimes you actually cop out on purpose. If you convince yourself that you'll never be any good at something because you're not "the type," what have you created? A really handy excuse for not even trying! Why should you even study for this English test — you're not the type of person who understands that stuff. Might as well be a foreign language to you.

This same attitude is particularly easy to adopt with God, with religion. You've probably even heard it before: "I believe in God and all, you know; and I don't have anything against religion, I mean it's fine for people who like it, but me, well, that's just not me — I'm not exactly the religious type, you know what I mean?"

Instantly you seem to be off the hook: no more church, no more praying, no more worry about rights and wrongs. Since you're not the religious type, you're free of religious obligations — right?

Of course not. But you might con yourself into thinking that.

This handy little gimmick can also be taken a step further. For example, you can have "Born to raise hell!" tatooed on your arm and then use it to excuse any hell-raising you feel like doing. You simply point to your tatoo and say, 'See? That's how I am. Not *my* fault I cause trouble. That's just the way I was made. My dad was the same way. Runs in the family."

There are lots of similar, very handy (and very empty) excuses. The excuses are endless:

• I was born with a hot tempter. It runs away with me and I feel bad about it sometimes, but I just can't control it.

98

- I was born with a crooked tongue. I couldn't tell the truth if I wanted to. I don't *like* to tell lies, but they just come out.
- I was born with this super strong sex drive. Hot blood, know what I mean? And if that's the way I am, well, that's the way I am. Nothing I can do about it.
- I was born hating blacks/whites/Jews/people of certain types. Even if paid to get along with them, I couldn't do it.

If something about religion turns you off, there are reasons for that. Some of them might be your responsibility; others might be the fault of people who didn't represent God very well to you. It's something you ought to look into and try to sort out.

But it's not because you were born into a little cell marked, "Not the Religious Type."

38. The Angel Norman Report

Norman guides his CTTM (Celestial-Terrestrial Travel Module) down toward the parking area of the Hillside Plaza Shopping Center. He wasn't particularly enthusiastic about this assignment to interview human beings and wished the Lord had chosen some other angel for the job. Earth creatures were . . . well, they certainly weren't angels. Norman sometimes wondered what the Lord saw in them.

He surveyed an empty parking slot. He had to descend quickly into it and deactivate the invisibility shield before another driver filled the spot. After he parked the CTTM, it materialized into a metallic blue van. Written on each side in customized, calligraphic lettering were the words:

Blest are they who hunger and thirst for holiness;
they shall have their fill (Matthew 5:6).

Norman himself materialized into a twenty-five-year-old man in a blue, pin-stripe suit. Taking a ballpoint pen and a clipboard, he set up his location on the busy sidewalk. He felt a little nervous. Human beings were unpredictable.

"Excuse me, sir," he said to the first man who passed, "we're doing a survey of opinions about holiness."

"Holiness? You mean like saints and all that kind of stuff?"

"Uh . . . yes. 'All that kind of stuff.' Exactly."

"Well, I think holiness is a very fine thing," the man said firmly. "In fact, there should be more of it. Much more of it, definitely."

"Wonderful," said Norman. "And are you yourself working toward holiness: (A) constantly and wholeheartedly; (B) fairly much; (C) sort of; (D) once in a while; or (E) not at all?"

"Well now, wait a minute," the man replied. "You asked my *opinion* of holiness. Like I said, I think it's a very fine thing and I'm in favor of it. But *being* holy — look I'm the sporting goods manager at a department store, plus I've got a family. I don't have time to work at holiness."

The man hurried away. Norman took his clipboard and made a note.

"Holiness?" gasped a girl about fifteen. "You . . . you *are* kidding, aren't you? I mean, this has got to be some kind of — are you from 'Candid Camera'?"

"No, I'm from — well, that's not important. I take it you think holiness is silly."

"Not exactly silly," the girl said. "It might be okay if it wasn't so boring."

"Holiness is boring?" Norman asked.

"You got it. With a capital B. I might try it later — like, a *lot* later. For now, I want to get some fun out of life. After all, you only go around once."

"You got *that* right," Norman sighed.

"Holiness?" said a college student. "I . . . well . . . see, I used to be into that, I really was. At least I thought I was. I mean, I prayed pretty much, did penance, even gave money to the missions — stuff like that. It was kind of neat at the time."

"What about now?" Norman asked.

"Well, you know how it is. You begin something sometimes and then you get sort of . . . sidetracked. Lose touch with it."

"But you can always start over, can't you?"

"Well, I guess I could. But I've already lost so much ground, know what I mean? It's like being out of shape. It seems dumb to start all over from the beginning and expect to be really good at it."

"I don't have to give my name, do I?" a ninth grade student asked.

"Of course not."

"Well, I made a retreat at school last year. You know, that's where you go somewhere different and think about stuff and. . . . "

"I'm with you," Norman said. "This retreat really got you into holiness, huh?"

"Well, yes and no. A lot of the things I heard made sense, you know? And — listen, if you tell this to anybody, I'll come looking for you — I sort of got turned on to this idea of holiness. I really did. I'm kinda sorry it won't work out."

"It won't? Why not?"

"You're putting me on! Look, I don't follow the crowd all the time, but I don't work at being strange, either."

"So you're concerned about what your peers think and you feel that holiness would make you strange."

"That's it."

Norman sighed, scribbled a few more notes, and stepped back into the van. He began to write his report.

"Earth creatures experience considerable confusion regarding holiness. Some think it's only for a few special people, or that it can't be worked into their regular lives. Many are convinced that even a little holiness will keep them from having fun; they think they have to choose between being holy or enjoying life. Some give up on holiness after a few setbacks. Others are frightened away from it by a terrible fear that holiness will turn them into freaks. All of this is, to use one of their own phrases, a pile of garbage, but they believe it anyway. Extensive retraining in the concept of holiness is badly needed on Earth."

39. Name That (Holy) Critter

Good evening game show fans and welcome once again to "The Prize Is In Sight!" It's time to meet our panel of contestants who have been chosen for their ability to scream, cry, jump thirty inches off the ground from a standing start, and act generally hysterical.

Contestant Number 1 is Paul Parkinson from Vian, Oklahoma, where Paul is a toaster installer. Paul, you'll get fifty points for a correct answer to this question: Name a mythical creature that never really existed — but people like to think it did because it makes for cute, inspirational stories.

"A unicorn!"

Correct and fifty points for Paul! Contestant Number 2 is Linda Brown from Spooner, Wisconsin, where she is a sidewalk crack counter. Linda, name a creature that used to live long ago but has died out.

"A dinosaur!"

Also correct and Linda comes even with Paul at fifty points!

Here's Contestant Number 3, Sandra Springs, who is a needle sharpener from Pliny, West Virginia. Sandra, name a creature that may or may not exist — some people say yes, some say no.

"Bigfoot — or the Loch Ness Monster!"

Another correct answer and we have three contestants at fifty points! Finally, here's Rick Maize from Cheviot, Ohio, where Rick is a chili parlor technician. Rick, name a creature that exists but is endangered — there are extremely few left.

"The snow leopard."

And Rick makes it a four-way tie after round one!

Notice that the contestants in this game show scene gave different answers for each of the four clues. But can you think of one single answer that would fit each of those clues, at least according to different people? A creature that: (1) never really existed but sounds cute; (2) lived long ago but disappeared; (3) may or may not be real; (4) still exists but is endangered — not many left.

A saint.

For some people, unfortunately, the word "saint" brings a picture of an almost unreal character. "Saint: a person who wore a long robe and a long face a long time ago and was somehow too good to be true."

Maybe you have this image because when you hear about saints you usually hear only the bottom line: their holiness. The lives of saints usually mention only their great accomplishments and glorious virtues. Maybe that's to be expected, but it can make you think that here was this unreal creature who was into holiness from the time he or she was wheeled around in a baby buggy (with a "Honk if you love Jesus" bumper sticker on the back). Saints started in the holiness business at "fantastic" and worked up from there.

And then you think, "Forget it. That's not me." Even worse, you may decide that sin is the norm and holiness is freaky.

Saints are not made more believable by merely recounting how good they were. Holiness isn't something you get zapped with, and once you get zapped with it: (1) doing the right thing is a piece of cake and (2) you're a little strange. (True, some of the saints had odd personalities, but holiness didn't cause that. There are tons of unsaintly people with odd personalities, too.)

Perhaps you have heard it said that "Saints were normal people who simply put God first and did their best at whatever their jobs were." And then you would think, "There's got to be a lot more to it than that." It is true, then, that saints didn't get their holiness handed to them like an inheritance, and they didn't always do everything right, like a little wind-up Mr. or Ms. Perfect Doll.

If the saints of the past are meaningful to you, they'll be an inspiration, but that doesn't mean you have to be exactly like them in all ways. You might read the works of Ernest Hemingway or the young adult novels of S. E. Hinton or Robert Cormier and feel a desire to write a novel of your own. You might get inspired by reading of their efforts to revise and polish a manuscript until it's as good as it can be. All wonderful.

But if you sit down and try to *write exactly like* Hemingway or Hinton or Cormier, if you try to create a novel that sounds like one of them might have written it, it's going to turn out awful. You're *not* any of them. To be a good writer, you have to write like you, not like somebody else.

About twenty-five years ago, a very wise man named Thomas Merton wrote, "For me to be a saint means to be myself." And who are "you"? The person God had in mind when he created you. Which is not the same person God had in mind when he created somebody else, particularly not somebody who lived in a different time and culture.

And real saints, as you may have guessed, don't fit *any* of those descriptions presented in the opening game show.

40. Hanging In When It Gets Tough

"Blest are those persecuted for holiness' sake;
  the reign of God is theirs" (Matthew 5:10).

Persecuted? All those Roman soldiers and invading barbarians have gone to their graves. Lions these days are either roaming their natural habitats or they're in zoos. They're not in amphitheaters devouring Christians (and intimidating more Christians who haven't been busted yet).

But other creatures have taken their place.

"Whaddya mean you don't want a joint or some crack? Anybody cool gets stoned and flies at least once in a while. Maybe you oughta go home to Mommy."

"Not give us the answers? Why not? You think you're better than everybody else or something — you want all the good grades for yourself? You got the answers, other guys need 'em, it's simple. Any of us would do it for *you*."

"*Everybody's* comin'! *Everybody's* in! You chicken or something? No guts, right?"

The situation is this: You're saying "*no*" when other people are saying "yes." You don't want to _____ when everybody else does. (Fill the blank with whatever fits.)

Or perhaps you've committed the almost unpardonable crime: You told an adult about something going on because you knew that was the right thing to do to keep somebody from getting hurt. There was a bust and you're considered the cause of it, even though it might have happened sooner or later anyway.

Whatever the case, the revenge starts. It's called "Making life miserable for the rat" or "Kicking the jerk out of the group."

Sometimes it's direct: You get hateful phone calls or rotten notes or both. Your locker gets torn up. Your bike gets a little wasted. The history notebook you need to study from is suddenly missing.

Sometimes it's indirect and subtle. You're not told when the group goes anywhere. You're not invited to anything or called about anything.

You come up to the group and it closes in and you're standing outside it, behind shoulders. Or you stand there in the group and it's like you're invisible; nobody looks at you or responds to anything you say.

It might last a week or it might last several months. It's the price you're paying for doing the right thing. And even though Jesus said you're "blest" for being in that situation, it can be awfully hard to feel that way. You're likely to feel a lot more rejected and hassled than blessed.

It hurts even more because you did the *right* thing. It's one thing to be punished for doing something wrong, but being punished for doing the right thing — that stinks.

But Jesus predicted it. It's one of the things he said that doesn't usually hit the popularity charts. Like it or not, he did say that if you really follow him, you're going to take some flak for it now and then.

That's when being Christian doesn't feel very much like peace and joy and alleluia and big banners proclaiming "LOVE" in bright felt lettering. That's when being a Christian means hanging tough in the face of pain and rejection.

And through it all, if you don't feel incredibly blessed . . . well, I guess that's why they call it faith. And remember that when the apostles went out to preach Jesus, they told people that they were bringing them the good news of salvation. They didn't say, "We come to bring you a piece of cake."

SECTION THIRTEEN:
LET'S TRY
TO BRING IT
ALL TOGETHER

41. For Ever and Ever. Amen.

"Dear God: Thank you for a pretty nice day and the ice cream. It was good, but I like chocolate better. I hope you saw me eat all my broccoli. Mommy said that made you happy. I hope it did because broccoli is sick. Please don't make it rain tomorrow because we're supposed to go to Kings Island. Bless my mommy and daddy and our dog and parakeet and make my brothers and sisters be nicer. And make me a good boy/girl so I can go to heaven."

There was a time when you may have said some prayers like that. They may sound silly now, but they weren't really. It's not silly to be whatever age you are.

But a lot of things have changed since the time a prayer like that seemed natural and appropriate. In particular, your understanding of things has changed. You know that dogs and parakeets do not need to be blessed. You know that God and your parents care about your health, but broccoli isn't necessarily a major element in God's cosmic plan.

Most of all, you now realize that God isn't going to make you into a good person in the sense that he'll force you to be good whether you want to or not. Over the past few years, you've probably noticed a definite lack of thunderbolts coming down at you from heaven. You're perfectly free to be a saint or a real jerk, as you choose.

A few questions may have crossed your mind on this right/wrong matter that we call "morality." These are questions that didn't occur to you back when you were asking God to bless the dog and the parakeet.

"How do you really know what's right and what's wrong?"

"Who says? How do they know?"

"Does it make any difference? People do lots of stuff that's supposed to be wrong, but nothing happens."

"If you think something is OK, then it *is* OK for you, right?"

"How do you learn right from wrong? Do you read and study it, or do you have to find out from experience?"

This book has tried to present some ideas that are helpful in making moral decisions. Morality is important; how people act makes a difference. If you don't believe that, you may as well go join a tribe of baboons.

But remember this: what is and isn't sinful is not the only part of being a Christian. Some people give you that impression. Just mention the word "religion" to them and they whip out a list of 7,843 things that are wrong to do and start reciting them at you. That's the old mistake of taking a part of the truth and treating it as though it were *all* there is to the truth.

Being a Christian starts with accepting and appreciating the absolutely incredible but true good news: You're a child of God, he's just crazy about you, and he wants to share a happiness with you that you've never dreamed possible. He wants this happiness for you so badly that when it was spoiled by sin, he sent the Son, Jesus, who was born into this world, died on a cross, and rose again to make things right again.

Over the centuries, people have come up with some very fancy, technical words for those ideas — words like "salvation" and "redemption" and "justification." That's fine. Technical words are necessary to help sort out some fine points when they need sorting out.

But the technical words still say the same fantastic things: God made you (when he didn't have to) and he made you different from dogs and orangutans. He loves you; he saved you from your own sinfulness.

So morality isn't a set of rules you're told to keep: If you don't break too many of them, you'll turn out to be a worthwhile human being and one of God's saved children. Morality makes you realize, "Hey, I'm a human being, a person. And that's pretty great. It's better than being a glob of granite or a miniature poodle. So I should act like a person."

And morality continues, "I am a specially created, saved child of God. Since that's what I am, that's how I should act."

In other words, you aren't just handed an instruction book along with the advice, "Here, kid — this is the book of training rules and game patterns. Memorize it, follow it, work, sweat, grind it out, keep your nose clean, and at the end maybe God will let you on his team."

It's more like this: "You made it, kid — welcome to the team! Happy to have you. You're asking *how* you made the team? Well, God said so, that's how. He likes you a lot.

"Anyway, you're officially a winner and great things are in store for you. Some of them are fun, some of them pretty routine, some of them difficult, but all of them worthwhile. You'll need to learn what the team is all about and how you should act. You'll make some mistakes, but there's help available so you can grow and learn from your mistakes.

"And wait till you see the post-season party! There's a permanent lease on this great place called heaven, and the celebration will go on *forever!* The only way this could turn out bad is if you keep opposing completely what the team is all about. If you do that and keep it up, well . . . you will have removed yourself from the team.''

Learning ''what you're all about'' as a person, as a saved child of God, is a big project. You start with this basic idea: There is such a thing as right and wrong. That may seem stupidly obvious, but some so-called educators have tossed out the idea of sin as outdated. Actions, they say, are not *sinful* — they are merely ''less appropriate'' or ''unwise.''

Holy smokescreen! That's like looking at a shirt smeared with grease and saying, ''Well, now, this shirt is not *really* dirty. To call it that might hurt somebody's feelings. Besides dirt is an outdated idea. This shirt is just 'less socially acceptable' than some other shirts.''

That idea is obviously attractive and lots of people buy into it. After all, it's nice to be told that there's really no such thing as actual right and wrong. It seems to get you out of a lot of responsibilities.

OK, if there is such a thing as right and wrong, where do you find out about it? There are two very different approaches to this.

One would say, ''In books. It's all right here — we have it all written down in books and church documents. We have all human actions labeled, categorized, divided, and subdivided. All you have to do is look it up.''

An opposite approach says, ''You can't go to a book to find out right from wrong. Even other people don't help that much. You learn right from wrong by living and then reflecting on your experience. After all, your life is not the same as anybody else's.''

There's something good in both these approaches, even though each is rather narrow by itself. The first one puts almost all the value on past human experience and the judgment of wise people. That has a lot going for it. People's lives may be somewhat different, but they're also similar in many ways. And some things really don't change, even from one century to the next. The surroundings people live in may be drastically different but people are still people — that doesn't change.

So in learning right from wrong it doesn't make any sense at all to ignore what other people have learned from their own experiences through the centuries. That would be like setting out to build an automobile but refusing even to read a book on basic mechanics and refusing even to let someone show you how to use a wrench.

Most important, Jesus didn't tell his apostles, ''Just go out and mention my name to people, and let them take it from there.'' He said, ''Teach them to carry out everything I have commanded you'' (Matthew

28:20). To call yourself a follower of Jesus and a member of his Church but decide that right and wrong is totally a do-it-yourself project . . . well, you can tell something is out of sync there.

At the same time, human life and experience is too varied, changing, and complicated to be completely described and labeled in books. Circumstances or conditions do change the morality of some actions and make it impossible to apply the exact same moral rule in exactly the same way one hundred percent of the time.

Culture can make a big difference. For example, styles of dress that are considered normal in some places would be a deliberate sexual advertisement and invitation in other places. So you can't define modesty once and for all by the total square inches of fabric a person is wearing.

Situations can make a difference. If your friend's father asks where his son or daughter is, you have an obligation to tell him. But if the father is drunk and you know he really beats the kid up when he's drunk, do you still have the same obligations? Of course not.

Often it's a combination of general, unchanging rules applied to the differing conditions of individual situations. The common thread running through all of it is the *value of persons* — of God, first of all, and of human beings. *All* human beings, not just those you think are cool.

And these rules of right and wrong aren't there to keep people from having fun. They're not merely a test of loyalty either: If you're tough enough to keep them, God will reward you with heaven. (Sort of like if your dog sits still for a while, you'll give it a doggie biscuit.)

Laws are there to protect the value and rights of persons. When the values and rights of persons are respected, life works pretty well. When they're not, life goes sour.

Those who say, "Nobody can *make* you believe something," are right. Nobody can make you take the Christian life seriously. Up to a certain age, parents and some other adults can control your behavior in certain ways, but not for long. No human being can force you to act in a certain way. And God chooses not to; that's just not his style.

So it really is your ball game. At least in the sense that you can play it in whatever way you choose — for a while. But sooner or later you have to deal with the setup of the ball field because *you can't change the way things are just by tuning them out*. Sooner or later you have to deal with the results of how you've acted during your time here on earth. Nobody comes into life with an entrance ticket that says, "Do whatever you want, whatever turns you on . . . there are no consequences."

You grow morally, or at least you should. Growth is often confusing and sometimes downright painful. Sometimes you seem to go backward before you're able to go forward. Sometimes you seem stuck in one spot and it looks as though you'll be there forever. Sometimes you may wonder if it's worth the effort and hassle of starting over again.

It's OK to be a little uncertain. God has made human life pretty complex. It wasn't simple even back in caveman days, and it's gotten steadily more complicated ever since. If somebody tells you that he or she has life completely and totally figured out, you begin to get a little worried about that person.

You're not bad or inferior or abnormal if the whole business of God and religion isn't as clear to you as the alphabet. But don't give it up and toss it out for that reason either. If something is difficult to understand, that doesn't make it stupid. Very often that's what makes it good. You just have to be willing to hang in and give it some effort.

So hang in there. Please. If you ever think, "This whole religion stuff was maybe just invented by an unbalanced, prehistoric cave dweller," hang in. Give yourself and God some time to work it out.

If you ever think, "God and religion are probably for real, but I keep failing, so why should I try?" hang in. You're right about one thing: *You* can't do it. But *you and God* can. Ask for help and keep asking.

If you ever think, "I'm already too far gone from what I'm supposed to be," hang in. One of the first complaints about Jesus is that he hung around with prostitutes, thieves, and an all-around miserable class of people. If Jesus could show them the way to a better life, he can handle anything you've done.

If you ever think, "Maybe I'll never do anything bad enough to rot in hell, but I can't cut being a real saint either, so I'll just sort of get by and settle for barely making it to heaven," hang in. Don't underestimate what you and God can do together.

A couple years ago, a kid I know was going through a pretty rough time in many ways. I couldn't solve the problems for him, and at the time I wasn't even sure exactly how he felt about what was going on. So I just sent him a note that said, "Hang in — we can't afford to lose you. Love, Jim."

I'd like to end this book with the same message, even if you're not going through a rough time right now.

Hang in with living the Christian life. We can't afford to lose you. Hope to see you all at the post-season celebration.

Love,

Jim